A SKETCH OF

Sam Bass,

THE BANDIT

A Sketch of
SAM BASS,
The Bandit

A GRAPHIC NARRATIVE

*His Various Train Robberies, His Death, and
Accounts of the Deaths of His Gang
and Their History*

[BY CHARLES L. MARTIN]

With an introduction by
RAMON F. ADAMS

UNIVERSITY OF OKLAHOMA PRESS

Norman

Library of Congress Catalog Card Number: 56-5991

New edition copyright 1956 by the University of Oklahoma Press,
Publishing Division of the University. Printed at Norman, Oklahoma, U.S.A., by the University of Oklahoma Press. First printing.

Contents

Contents

Illustrations

THE LAST FIGHT.

Introduction

DURING THE short criminal career of Sam Bass, and immediately afterward, there were four books written about him, all now exceedingly rare. This book by Charles Lee Martin was the last of the quartet and has become one of the rarest. Personally I know of but one copy of the original, and that is in the Library of Congress.

For some reason all but one of these four books were published anonymously. Perhaps it was because they were written during the life of Bass and his followers and there was some fear of retaliation, but more likely it was because the writers were too proud to have their names associated with that of an outlaw. In those days the paper-backed books about outlaws were classed with the "penny dreadfuls" forbidden to youngsters and read in secret by adults. To be known as the author of such a book did not improve one's literary reputation or his standing in the community. Therefore, most authors of such wrote under a pseudonym.

The first of these anonymous books was written by Thomas E. Hogg, whose brother was later governor of Texas. It was published in Denton, Texas, in 1876, under the by-line, "by a citizen of Denton County, Texas." Because the author was a member of the posse which chased Bass all over Denton County, he told some things firsthand. A first edition of this book is now practically unprocurable, although it has been reprinted, once by the

A Sketch of Sam Bass, the Bandit

Frontier Times in 1926 after it had been run serially in that little magazine, and again by these same publishers in 1932 in a "Museum Edition" with a different format and with eleven pages added by the publishers.

In 1877, Alfred Sorenson was bold enough to publish under his own name a book dealing with Sam Bass. This is another exceedingly rare book published in wrappers with the title *"Hands Up!" or, the History of a Crime. The Great Union Pacific Express Robbery.* The original edition was published in Omaha by the Barkalow brothers, and it was later reprinted by C. B. Dillingham of New York, though I have never seen a copy of the latter edition.

"Hands Up" was published immediately after the Union Pacific robbery took place and is devoted almost entirely to this crime. It gives the most complete and detailed account of it yet written. It tells of the killing of Collins and Heffridge, and ends a little later with the killing of Berry in Mexico, Missouri. All of Bass's Texas criminal activities occurred after this book was published. It was also included in condensed form in a chapter of the author's later book *The Story of Omaha, from Pioneer Days to the Present Time.*

The third book on Sam Bass was also published anonymously in Dallas, Texas, by the Dallas Commercial Steam Print in 1878, under the title, *Life and Adventures of Sam Bass* . . . . No one seems to know the author of this work. Copies of the first edition seem to have disappeared, also, though there are some reprints still occasionally found in rare-book dealers' catalogs. The most common of these reprints is the one published by John A. Norris, of Austin, Texas, issued in blue wrappers. It was later reprinted by H. N. Gammel, of Austin, and issued in tan wrappers. Although the original contained illustrations, neither of these reprints retained them. The latest reprint of this book was made by the Frontier Press, of Houston, Texas, in 1952, and contains new illustrations from the famous Rose Collection.

This Bass book is similar to the one written by Hogg in 1876, for there was nothing much new to add since both got their information from living eyewitnesses and contemporary newspaper accounts.

This brings us to the last of the quartet of rare books on Sam Bass, herewith being reprinted for the first time. When we consider that all the other books of this group have been reprinted, I think the University of Oklahoma Press is to be commended for bringing this book—the rarest of the lot—within the reach of those interested, who would likely never see a copy of the original.

This particular book, too, was published anonymously, but the author did write his name as "Charles L. Martin" in pen and ink on the title page of the copy he sent to the copyright office. It was published in Dallas, Texas, by the Herald Steam Printing House in 1880, two years after Bass's death. But because it was published in Dallas, it should not be confused with the other one published in this city two years earlier.

Martin's account is substantially the same as the others, but in a long chapter entitled "The Band," he gives a more extended and more accurate biography of the members of the Bass gang, such as Henry Underwood, Seaborn Barnes, and "Arkansaw" Johnson, and scattered throughout the book is some information not found elsewhere.

It might be of interest to know something of the author of this little book and of the artist who illustrated it. Charles Lee Martin was a native Texan, born in San Augustine, March 6, 1835, the third anniversary of the fall of the Alamo. During his colorful life he was a soldier, lawyer, and editor, and his career extended back to the days when Texas was a republic.

His father came to Texas from Mississippi and his mother from Virginia. His father successfully ran a steamboat line between Jefferson and New Orleans from 1849 to 1861, re-entering the business after the Civil War and continuing until the railroads killed river navigation.

Charles attended the Marshall schools until 1856, when he started his college career at Franklin College, near Nashville, Tennessee, which he attended for a year. In 1857 he went to the Kentucky Military Institute, graduating on June 28, 1860. Two years before his graduation he was elected to membership in Delta Kappa Epsilon, and in later years was spoken of as the oldest Greek-letter man in the United States. At K.M.I. he won honors in both his junior and his senior years and was valedictorian of his class.

Just a few days before his graduation he married Miss Mary Lindsey, of Bourbon, Kentucky. With his bride he returned to his home in Marshall, Texas, and entered the firm of Pope and Willie to practice law. The following December he moved to Guadalupe County, to which he had to travel by stagecoach.

At the outbreak of the Civil War, he returned to Marshall and entered the Confederate Army as first lieutenant, serving four years as a commissioned officer of the Confederacy.

The war over, he returned to Texas and tried farming in Grimes County for a year, but when his crops were ruined by hailstorms, he went back to the practice of law, serving a part of four years as acting county attorney.

In 1869 he made his home in Jefferson, Texas, but with the city under martial law at the time, the courts were closed, so he went back to steamboating with his father through 1870. The following year he resumed his law practice, serving as city attorney for more than a year and as county attorney for two years.

In 1873 he quit the practice of law to enter the field of journalism. After serving for a time as the first editor of the *Jefferson Tribune*, he moved to Houston, where he joined the *Houston Mercury* as an editorial writer under Joseph Wilson.

Later he became city editor of the *Houston Age*, and still later of the *Houston Telegraph*. He moved to Dallas in 1878, the year Sam Bass was killed, and wrote editorials for the *Morning Call*. It was at this time that he became interested in the career of Bass. Later he went to the *Dallas Herald* in the same capacity. In the latter part of 1885 he again went to Houston, to accept the city editorship of the *Houston Post*, but returned to Dallas the following year, where he remained until his death. On this last move to Dallas he worked for a time for the Western Newspaper Union, later becoming editor of the *Dallas Evening Herald*.

He wrote prolifically on a wide variety of subjects and pursued his hobby of Texas history until he was called the "walking encyclopedia of Texas." When we compare his other subjects with this book, we can see why he chose to write anonymously of Sam Bass.

He joined the staff of the *Dallas Morning News* in 1887, where he remained until his eyesight failed in 1900. After years of treatment he returned to his desk in 1909 and remained until his death on November 24, 1925. At the time of his death he was writing a history of the Confederate Navy.

Sam Bass was illustrated by Stephen Seymour Thomas, who was also born in San Augustine, Texas, August 20,

1868, the son of James Edwards and Mary Landron (Blount). A student at Art Students' League from 1885 to 1888, he went to Paris to attend the Académie Julien from 1888 to 1891, where he was a pupil of Jules Lefebre and Benjamin Constant. On October 11, 1892, he married Helen M. Haskell. Much later, in 1914, he received his Master of Arts degree from Williams College.

He exhibited pictures at the Cotton Centennial Exposition at New Orleans when he was only sixteen years old, having earlier, at the age of twelve, drawn the illustrations for this book on Sam Bass. During his lifetime he painted portraits of many famous and prominent people, won world-wide recognition, and received many honors and medals. Little did the author of this outlaw "thriller" foresee that his young illustrator would become a famous person.

This last of the quartet of books written about Sam Bass, all within a period of five years, is perhaps the most thorough, the longest, and the rarest. It seems strange that the majority of these outlaw books could become so scarce during the course of a few years, but it must be remembered that they were usually printed on cheap paper and received rough treatment in reading. Most of them sold for about twenty-five cents, and as this class of literature was not considered very elevating in those days —and the book not one a man would care to exhibit on his library shelves—they were often read and thrown away—usually into the fire.

Sam Bass was not much of an outlaw as outlaws go. He was no gunman, nor was he a killer. In fact, he seemed to have refrained from killing his fellow-men and kept his followers from doing so. In studying his history, we find that his gang had many gun battles in the course of being chased by posses of Denton County. Yet in all this shooting Bass and his men seemed to be merely trying to hold off the posse by near misses until they could escape.

At Round Rock, Bass seemed to know he was in a tight spot and perhaps shot to kill for the first time in his career. And now that he had done so, it meant his own death. No one knows whose bullet killed Grimes, but his death broke up the Bass gang. Nor does anyone know for sure whose bullet was the fatal one for Bass. Some historians claim it was fired by Ranger George Harrell, others say by Ranger Dick Ware. However, more recently, Highsmith, the liveryman, behind whose stable most of the shooting took place, has told investigators that the fatal shot was fired by another Ranger who stood beside him and fired the one shot. The Ranger then told Highsmith that he had nothing against Sam Bass and cautioned Highsmith not to mention his name in connection with the killing.

In my personal library I have approximately two hundred books that deal with Sam Bass or devote some space to him. His popularity as an outlaw is growing with the years. The song written about him is a favorite with the cowhand and has been sung from one end of the trail to the other, thus having a significant influence on his popularity. Also, it is well known that Sam Bass was a hail-fellow-well-met, never vicious, a lover of good horses, true to his friends, and generous with his money. Anyone who loves a good horse stands high in the esteem of a Westerner. It is said that Frank Jackson joined Bass's gang just to have an opportunity to ride his Denton mare, which had some reputation as a race horse.

Many of the books in my library, like most books dealing with our early outlaws, contain errors of historical fact.

A Sketch of Sam Bass, the Bandit

E. C. "Teddy Blue" Abbott, in his *We Pointed Them North,* makes the statement that Bass was his father's wagon boss before he went to Texas. Since Bass went to Denton, Texas, while yet in his teens and had never had any experience with cattle, this is obviously a case of bad memory or confusion.

A little pamphlet published by the Sam Bass Cafe' of Round Rock, Texas, in 1929, gives a condensed account of Bass, allegedly written from the Adjutant General's files by the son of a Texas Ranger. Though hitting only the high spots of Bass's career, it contains many errors—such as that the Union Pacific robbery netted the robbers $65,000, and that the Eagle Ford robbery was the first committed by the Bass gang in Texas. The latter happened to be the third train robbery since Bass's return to Texas.

Ed F. Bates, in his *History and Reminiscences of Denton County,* is also incorrect in his account of the Union Pacific robbery. And Murphy did not break jail at Tyler, Texas, but skipped bond in a frameup arranged with the officers so that he might return to the gang and betray his friend Sam Bass. Nor did the killing of Grimes at Round Rock occur in a saloon, but in Henry Koppel's store, where the gang had gone to purchase tobacco.

E. Douglas Branch, in his *The Cowboy and His Interpreters,* is also confused about the amount of money involved in the Union Pacific robbery, stating that the gang got $5,000 from the passengers and $15,000 from the express car. Many writers have given various amounts netted in this robbery, Robert J. Casey, even as late as 1950, in *The Texas Border,* citing the amount as $75,000 instead of $60,000. Lewis S. Delong, in his *Forty Years a Peace Officer,* makes the preposterous statement that John Selman killed Sam Bass; and Jay Donald, in his scarce *Outlaws of the Border,* has both Bass and Bill Longley members of the James gang.

N. Wilson Rankin, in *Reminiscences of Frontier Days,* is mistaken in his statement that Joel Collins and Sam Bass fled to the Indian Territory after the Union Pacific robbery, and that they were later arrested and sentenced to a prison term.

This list could be greatly extended, but I have discussed the subject more thoroughly in another work.[1]

It remained for Wayne Gard, editorial writer of the *Dallas Morning News,* to write the most complete and accurate biography of Sam Bass yet published. Published in 1936, it has long been out of print and had never been reissued. It is regrettable that such a book was allowed to go out of print so soon. I believe I have read every book written about Sam Bass, and all of those containing any information on him, and I can safely say that Mr. Gard's book is the only one giving any worthwhile information concerning Bass's ancestry and early boyhood. It also contains much information not found in other places and goes more into detail than any other book on Bass before or since.

None of the earlier books mentioned deal with Bass's experiences in the Black Hills to any extent. They tell of a few stage robberies, then pass hurriedly to the Big Springs robbery of the Union Pacific.

The Dallas 1878 edition barely touches upon a stage robbery and fails to mention the killing of Johnny Slaughter. It also reports that Bass met Nixon and Jack Davis after he went to the Black Hills, while the Hogg edition has Jack Davis going up the trail from San Antonio with

---

[1] *Six-Guns and Saddle Leather: A Bibliography of Outlaws and Gunmen* (Norman, University of Oklahoma Press, 1954).

Bass and Collins and relates that they met Nixon, Heff-ridge, and Berry in the Black Hills.

Both the Hogg and the Martin books tell of the killing of Johnny Slaughter, though they do not mention him by name—merely designating him as a stage driver—and in both the killing is done by Collins and Heffridge, one on either side of the road during the attempted holdup.

In this, both authors are mistaken, for Slaughter was killed by Robert McKimie, better known by the name "Little Reddie." He joined the Collins gang in February, 1877, and was one of the leading spirits of the gang, though none of the early books on Bass mention him. Slaughter was well liked and one of the most popular drivers on the line, and his murder created much indignation. "Reddie" admitted to Mr. Voorhees, superintendent of the Black Hills and Cheyenne Stage Company, that he fired the shot, but claimed his gun went off accidently. Whether it was an accident or not, the sawed-off shotgun in McKimie's hands was filled with buckshot, and its blast killed a man who had far more friends than enemies. Not only did this killing create great resentment among the law-abiding citizens, but it also caused the other members of the Collins gang to kick "Reddie" out because of his careless trigger finger.

The killing of Slaughter was first told in another exceed-ingly rare book entitled *The Life and Adventures of Robert McKimie, Alias "Little Reddie," from Texas. The Dare-Devil Desperado of the Black Hills Region, Chief of the Murderous Gang of Treasure Coach Robbers.* This volume was compiled by J. W. Bridwell and published by the *Hillsboro Gazette*, of Hillsboro, Ohio, in 1878. Although it does not mention Bass by name, it does tell of McKimie's joining the Collins gang and of the subsequent killing of Slaughter.

Introduction

Again, it remained for Wayne Gard to give us the most accurate account of this attempted robbery. Aside from the McKimie book, his is the only one to mention "Reddie" as being the killer of Slaughter, and Mr. Gard has the gang in this particular holdup composed of Collins, Bass, Towle, and "Reddie." Other authors say that Collins and Heffridge did the shooting, and none mention Towle and "Reddie" as members of the gang. In 1949, Agnes Wright Spring, in her excellent book, *The Cheyenne and Black Hills Stage and Express Routes,* also tells of McKimie's being in the Collins gang, though she spells the name "McKemma."

Many of the early writers were either careless with their geography, or perhaps they read no proofs in those days. The McKimie book speaks of M. F. Leach, the detective who got on the trail of the Union Pacific robbers, as being from Ogallala, *Missouri,* and Mr. Martin, in the book being introduced here, writes of Deadwood, *Idaho Territory!*

As a whole, however, I find Mr. Martin's book to be fairly accurate, and more thorough than those of his predecessors. Of course, Mr. Hogg could speak in the first person with authority when writing of the posse chasing Sam Bass from hide-out to hide-out, for he was a member of that posse, but Mr. Martin revealed his training as a lawyer and an editor in his thoroughness. It is perhaps on account of this book's rarity that it has not been reprinted before now, but it is undoubtedly one for which readers and collectors will be grateful.

RAMON F. ADAMS

Dallas, Texas
October 21, 1955

A SKETCH OF

Sam Bass,

THE BANDIT

CHAPTER I

The Boyhood of Bass

*He begins life for himself—His early adventures away
from home—He progresses in hoodlumism—
His entry into Texas*

THE HERO of our "over true tale," Sam Bass, first saw
the light in Indiana, he being a native of Lawrence
County in that state. He was born on the 21st day of July,
1851, on his father's farm, some two miles from the town
of Mitchell. His father, Daniel Bass, married his mother,
Elizabeth Sheeks, in 1840, and by industry, economy,
and sterling honesty he surrounded himself with the comforts of life, being the possessor of an excellent small farm,
well stocked. His parents had ten children born unto
them, the eldest two dying in their infancy. Sam's oldest
brother, George, entered the Union Army when the war
broke out between the states in 1861, and as a member
of the Sixteenth Indiana Regiment did good service for
his country until he was killed on the 30th of August,
1862, at the battle of Richmond, Kentucky. Excepting
Sam, who now slumbers in his bloody grave at Round
Rock, Williamson County, Texas, the rest of the children,
six in number, were at last accounts living in Indiana.
The names of those living are John Bass, Denton Bass,
Sallie Bass, Euphemia Beasly, Mary Hersey, and Clarissa
Hersey, and they are respectable people, enjoying the

esteem of their neighbors, and all doing well in the world.

Sam's mother died in 1861, when he was but ten years of age, leaving him a high-strung, mettlesome boy, without a mother's guiding precepts and restraining counsels. His father soon married again to a young widow devoted to piety and Methodism, she being a member of the Methodist church and prayed in public and lead in class meeting. He died February 20th, 1864, leaving a young widow and one child, the fruit of their marriage, Charles Bass, who now resides in Missouri. After the death of their father a maternal uncle of the Bass children, Daniel L. Sheeks, was made guardian of their estate and persons. He was a man of great respectability, in comfortable circumstances, and he trained the children while they were under his care in the way they should go and gave them the same educational advantages he did their cousins, his own children. Sam did not seem to profit much, however, by these advantages, for he could not read and was scarcely able to sign his own name.

Right here we again take occasion to say that there is no doubt that Sam Bass's family, both upon his father's and his mother's side, were people of respectability, people who stood well in the communities in which they lived, possessing the esteem and confidence of the public.

Up to the age of fifteen or sixteen years, Sam Bass conducted himself as an upright, well-behaved boy should and bore as good a character as any boy in his neighborhood. Soon after this, however, he chanced upon bad associates and began to follow evil ways and acquire disreputable habits.

When he was eighteen years of age, in 1869, his uncle's home grew irksome to him; he longed to see something of the great world about which he knew so little, and the

4

glamour of whose glories enticed his soul, until his heart grew fretful within him, and he left forever the peace and quietude and safety of the fold where his brothers and sisters still lingered. Leaving Indiana, he wandered off to St. Louis, that great, seething cauldron of vice and temptation. He remained in "The Future Great" but a short while, the attractions of city life failing to satisfy him; so he took passage on a steamer for the South, determined to seek for a fortune in this terra incognita to the western raised boy. In a few days the boat landed at Rosedale, Mississippi, where he disembarked and sought employment. After he had been at Rosedale about a week, he found a situation at a mill owned by a man named Charles, and worked there a year. His mill associations were not good for him, for his bad habits developed very rapidly, and he became an expert in gambling, learned how to shoot a six-shooter with the dexterity of a bandit, and could drink whisky with any toper.

Tiring of mill work and of Mississippi, he took his effects and departed for Texas in 1870, stopping in Denton County in the late fall of that year. The change seemed to have been morally beneficial to him, for he at once eschewed his former bad habits, forswore dissipation, and obtaining employment, he buckled down to hard work. Mrs. Lacy, proprietress of the Lacy House, in the town of Denton, was the first person who gave him a situation. He was faithful to her services for some eighteen months, being attentive to all the duties incumbent upon him, and by his good behavior and gentle qualities endearing himself to that good lady. He next went to work for a man named Wilkes, with whom he remained but a short time, when he entered the service of W. F. Eagan, sheriff of the county. He worked for Sheriff Eagan until 1874, driving a team and herding cattle, and doing whatever service that gentleman put him to. Sheriff Eagan says, up to a short time before he discharged him, Bass was sober, industrious, economical, and respectable in all ways. He was pleased with his services and had perfect confidence in him, frequently sending him to Dallas with large sums of money for the purchase of lumber and other things he needed. In fact Mr. Eagan says that he was so economical as to be almost parsimonious, and he had frequently to chide him for starving himself and the team he was driving. He would not wear any but the cheapest, plainest of clothing, but he was always devoted to his employer's interests and strove diligently to further his ends by his industry and fidelity. Of a retiring, reticent nature, he spent his Sundays and evenings closely at home, never leaving the place unless sent off, and he formed no companionships, associating with no person except a little boy in the town who taught him to write. The truth is, the young man seemed to have repented his early indiscretions and wild habits, and to have formed the determination to make a man of himself and be a good and respected citizen, as his father had been, and as all his relatives were. Alas! had he but clung to these resolves, his young life would not have been flung away in an infamous calling; he would not have filled the hearts of his sisters and brothers with a fearful anguish, and he would not have left behind him a name that only lives on the pages of shame and ignominy.

In 1874 Bass purchased "a little sorrel mare," as she is graphically described by those who knew him well, and then it may be said he entered upon that career which made him notorious and which put his name in the mouths of all men, and which brought down upon him the ire of the federal government and of the State of Texas. The mare, unfortunately, could run fast, and this tempted him to try his fortunes on the turf. After running a few successful races around Denton, Sheriff Eagan told him he must dispose of the mare or else give up his situation as his teamster. Sam was too enamored of his mare to part with her, and threw up his situation. He then, this being 1875, began a life of dissipation. The only business he followed was racing and gambling. His nights were spent in carousing and card playing, at which he was an adept, and his companions were only of the most dissolute, questionable character. About this time he formed the acquaintance of Henry Underwood, from whom he was inseparable, and who afterwards became his companion and the lieutenant of his noted gang of highwaymen. His neighbors say that after he began his dissipation he seemed entirely changed from his former self, and no doubt he was, for he seemed to have suddenly become possessed of a devil. Naturally of a headstrong disposition, and of a spirit that could brook no opposition or reverse, he went to the extreme of perversity and wild waywardness. His was just the character that develops into leading citizenship, leaving the impress of good on all around, or into a fiend incarnate, breaking down all the barriers of law and order, and riding rough-shod over society.

Early impressions are always lasting and leave their effects for good or evil on the heart according as they may be directed. When Sam was but a child less than ten years of age, he was present at a great criminal trial where he lived, and it seems to have left an impression upon the mind and heart that ripened mayhap into a desire for notoriety. Had that impression been used to show him the dire results, the woes of a criminal life, he might have been a different man from what he was. But whatever effect this criminal trial may have had upon his mind, he was heard to say one day in Denton after he had renounced his sober and industrious habits, on seeing some horse thieves being sent to the penitentiary, that when he "committed crime it would amount to something," that he "would never be sent to the penitentiary for so small a thing as stealing a horse." This remark showed that his ideas of what was a crime were not as clear and correct as they should have been, else he would not have considered horse thieves as small criminals.

CHAPTER II

His First Robbery

Trading in ponies—Horse racing at the Alamo City—
Sale of the race mare, and on the
cattle trail

BASS RAN horse races, played cards, drank whisky, and frolicked generally, for some months in and around Denton, after leaving the employ of Sheriff Eagan, when in the summer he and five or six companions left there and went to Fort Sill. He remained at the Fort for two or three months, but little is known of his career while there, though it is not suspected that he engaged in any enterprises other than his usual racing and gambling and dissipation.

When next he was heard of after leaving the Fort, he had gone down into the interior of the Indian Nation on a racing tour. He found no trouble in making races, for if there is anything an Indian delights in more than another, next to drinking whisky and scalping white people, it is horse racing, and the class of white men generally found in the Nation glory in any sort of sport, so matches were easy to get with his "little sorrel mare." They were short dashes, it is true, and the rules peculiar to jockey club courses were all dispensed with, and there were no niceties as to weight to be respected, nor tastes as to colors to be consulted, but there was always a crowd at the races, and bald-faced whisky, when it could be smuggled in, was drank freely, and the choicest oaths prevailed on every hand, until the air looked blue and a sulphurous smell seemed to pervade the atmosphere. Sam could always win the race, but he could not always get the stakes. The wagers on these races were invariably ponies, for the Indians had nothing else to bet, and as the stakes were only virtually up, getting possession of them was the rub. The Indians made their races to win. If they couldn't beat "the little sorrel mare," they could beat her owner by not delivering the ponies to him. It wasn't Sam's nature to stand this sort of treatment. He had won the ponies in a fair race, that is, as fair a race as could be run with an Indian, and he intended to have those ponies or know the reason why. Right there the first culmination of his evil course was reached. He could not reason the Indians out of the ponies; he could not persuade them to give them up; he could not curse them into it, nor scare them, so he determined to take them. Therefore, one favorable night, he rounded up all the ponies he had won, and as many more as he could gather, and made a break for Texas. Before morning he had crossed Red River and headed straight for San Antonio, Texas.

This is the first robbery of which Sam is known to have been guilty. Whether he ever stopped to ask himself if it was robbery or not, it is doubtful. He seems to have, by that time, overcome whatever scruples he might once have possessed, and if he considered all of his act at all, he doubtless reasoned that taking the ponies he had won was only taking his own property, and that he was entitled to the others for the delay the obstinacy of the Indians had caused him and to replace any of those he had won which might get away from him or die on his hands. In other

10

words, he was playing for even and he got even. It was one of his characteristics never to "get left" when he could help it.

Bass continued on across the state with his ponies to San Antonio, arriving at that place in December, 1875, just nine months after he left the services of Sheriff Eagan, at Denton. In that nine months he had developed into a confirmed gambler, a horse racer, a guzzler of whisky, a brawling desperado, a horse thief. Apt scholar he was in the school of crime. At San Antonio he disposed of the ponies, and engaged in his usual avocation of horse racing and card playing, with the accompaniment of whisky drinking.

San Antonio is almost a classic city. All about it cluster some of the brightest and saddest memories in the history of Texas. The gallant, chivalrous deeds of noble men, inspired with the loftiest sentiments of patriotism and love of liberty and justice, give lustre to its name. Romantic in all its surroundings, beautiful as it nestles amid its hills, beside its clear, gently flowing waters, the home of all classes, from the most exalted of the Anglo-Saxon race to the humblest and most degraded specimen of the Mexican, it is eminently a cosmopolitan city. There the Christian, the clergyman, and the sneak thief jostle each other on the narrow side walks; there the jurist renowned in the courts of the state and the most hardened criminal find a permanent and temporary abode; there the worthy citizen and the mountebank find labor to their hands. A congenial class could Sam Bass find in San Antonio, for the adventurer, the gambler, the cut-throat, the horse thief, all congregate in this frontier city, and here Sam Bass found congenial spirits.

Shortly after his arrival at San Antonio he formed the acquaintance of Joel Collins. As this man figured promi-

11

nently for a brief period in Bass' career, and his brothers also became implicated with Bass, it will not be amiss to say a few words about him here. He was born of a good family in Kentucky, was well educated, and reared a gentleman. Genial, whole-souled, and generous, he made friends wherever he went. At the time he met Bass in San Antonio he was living in Southwest Texas, engaged in stock raising and cattle trading. He had always borne a good character and there was nothing in the man that was inherently bad. A good many people believe that he led Sam Bass into deeds of robbery and desperadoism, but those who knew Joel Collins best believe that it was the other way, that he was the victim of Bass' seductive wiles. Be this as it may, he and Bass formed an acquaintance at San Antonio which soon ripened into a warm friendship.

There was nothing of special note that occurred during the several months they remained together in San Antonio. The usual routine of racing and gambling was vigorously pursued. They enacted their racing schemes with great shrewdness and unscrupulousness. The "little sorrel mare" was put in charge of Collins, and Bass played the role of horse trainer, inveigling himself into the good graces of every man who had a fast horse. Insinuating and persuasive, he would get charge of some horse, test its speed, and if he was satisfied the little mare could beat it, would induce the owner to make a race against Collins, and incite him and his friends to bet all the money they had on the result. The consequence was that he and Collins reaped a rich reward from the dupes. They squandered their money, however, nearly as fast as they made it. "Come easy, go easy," it was with them, and women and wine filled up the measure of their pleasures.

In August of 1876, Collins proposed to Bass that they

buy a herd of cattle and drive them to some of the Western states or territories for a market. They had a little money, and Collins being pretty well known in Southwest Texas, they succeeded, by paying part cash, in getting near five hundred beef steers. With this herd they started on the cattle trail for Kansas. With them was Jack Davis, another character who is to figure somewhat in this crude narrative of Bass's exploits. In Northwest Kansas they sold their cattle at a handsome profit, and if they had been honest, just men, they would have returned to Texas, paid the stock men who had trusted them, and have had a large margin in good money made on their venture. This would have enabled them to buy again the next season a larger herd, and thus they could have gone on, each year making more and more until wealth and affluence would have been theirs. But why moralize? Sam Bass was a thief in his heart, his true nature asserted itself, and fate for a brief period let him weed a row that led straight to the grave through the surroundings of infamy and disgrace.

Having sold their cattle, Bass and Collins, with Jack Davis as their boon companion, entered upon a course of gaming and carousing and "having lots of fun," until they ran through with about $5,000 of their money, when they left Kansas for Deadwood, in Idaho Territory.

CHAPTER III

Deadwood Dare Devils

*Teaming for a living don't pay—Stage robbing is not
much better but then it is livelier—A frontier
home and gay girls to share it*

ARRIVING AT Deadwood, Bass and Collins had about
$8,000 in money, or more properly speaking, perhaps,
Collins had about $8,000 and shared his funds with Bass
and Jack Davis. When they arrived at Deadwood, Joel
Collins, remembering that he was reared a gentleman,
remembering his old father and mother living in Dallas
County, Texas, as good people in every respect as ever
lived anywhere; remembering his brothers and sisters and
their standing in society; remembering the teachings of
his pious old mother when she taught him to pray at her
knee, when she advised with him in his childhood, in his
boyhood, in his youth, and in his early manhood, and
counseled him to walk always in the paths of rectitude and
of truth—remembering all these things and paying heed
to the admonitions of his conscience and of his better
nature, he made up his mind to change his evil ways and
try to be a better man. Inspired with this determination,
he said to Bass, "I believe, Sam, I'll build me a good house
here and quit our foolishness. I think I'll go to mining."
He proceeded to build him a house at a cost of $3,500,
and to furnish it in the most sumptuous style that country

14

would admit of. To it he carried his mistress—fatal error —a lewd siren named Maude, at this writing living in a den of infamy in the city of Dallas, and put her in charge of the premises, installed her as the deity of his household.

To carry into effect his good intentions of sobriety and industrious pursuits, he fitted out a wagon and team and started Bass to freighting between Deadwood City and Cheyenne. Sam's first trip brought him in debt $60. He then gave Jack Davis $250 and started him with a four-horse team to freighting between Deadwood City and Cheyenne. In a little time he returned without a cent of money and with only two horses. This was discouraging and he stopped the business in disgust.

His home was made a regular ranche. He had a "gay girl" to solace his hours, and Sam and Jack Davis had to have one each, too. What, with lasciviousness and dram drinking, the two and their inamoratas led a fearfully fast life. But everything comes to an end without money, and funds were running short. Some sort of venture must be made to increase the finances. To this end they got a few more girls of the same order as of those living with them, and they opened a regular brothel. To it they attached a saloon, and every night there was a dance. The country was full of miners, and their "ranche" soon became the most degraded den of infamy that ever cursed earth. Great God! what a fearful calling was theirs. How the angel mother of Sam Bass, from the battlements of Heaven, must have wept as she looked down upon him in his degradation and infamy, and how the heart of Joel Collins' old mother would have been torn with anguish had she known of her son's ignominious pursuits.

Despite the fact that they made money with their bagnio, they soon were in great straits for finances, because

15

they squandered and gambled off what they made as fast as it came in, and they were forced to shut up their shop. What next was to do was the question. About this time they formed the acquaintance of three desperadoes, three kindred spirits ready for anything that would give them excitement or bring them money, three hardened cases— Bill Heffridge, of Texas, Jim Berry, of Missouri, and Tom Nixon, from various places. These three enterprising young men had been boarding at "the ranche" a few weeks, and all hands had become very intimate. Finally they formed a joint stock company, the six of them, Bass, Collins, Davis, Heffridge, Berry, Nixon & Co., the company being the amiable and angelic Maude, Collins' evil genius, to go to stage robbing. The first thing to do was to mount themselves. This they quickly did, levying on horseflesh in the neighborhood, without regard to the rights of others.

Well, they proceeded at once to work. They stopped and went through a number of stage coaches and robbed several travelers on the highway, but in all their ventures they made only about $100. Finally they attempted to stop a stage, one day, when the driver not being complacent, put the whip to his horses and started on the run. Collins and Heffridge fired on the driver with their Winchester rifles, and he fell from his seat dead. The horses, of course, continued to run, and they followed after, shooting at them with the hopes of killing a horse and thus stopping the coach, but failing to do so they abandoned the chase, and the horses ran on into Deadwood City. The killing of the driver caused no little excitement, and being suspected of the murder, they found it to their advantage to keep in the background for a while. They separated, going in twos in different directions, but making Collins' ranche a place of rendezvous, where they would occasionally meet and through which they would communicate with each other. Finally, about the 1st of September, they all met at the ranche, and discussing the situation, Berry suggested that they leave that section of the country and go and rob a railroad train. He said he had never tackled a train, but he felt that he had it in him to do so successfully, and that he could form a plan whereby they could capture a pile from the express and the passengers on some east-bound train on the Union Pacific road. The motion being seconded, they made their arrangements to leave at once and enter upon their new field of exploits.

THE DEATH OF DEPUTY MARSHAL ANDERSON AND BILLIE COLLINS

CHAPTER IV

The First Big Steal

Going through a Union Pacific train—A successful haul
and the end thereof—Personelle of some of the
actors in this stupendous robbery

AFTER COLLINS, Bass, and their confederates had agreed
upon their future actions and determined to go to
train robbing, they, having stolen good horses for their
trip, left Deadwood City for the Union Pacific Railroad.
The party had only $40 in money between them, a small
amount indeed for men of as luxurious habits as they had
acquired and indulged in for a year or more past. In their
reduced financial condition they were ready for any enter-
prise, no matter what the nature or how desperate the
chances. Their experiences at Deadwood City had prepared
them for readiness in any employment. There is no better
way to give an idea of what they were capable of than to
give a chapter or two of Deadwood history, occurring in
the main during their sojourn in that remarkable city of
the Far West, a place where no man dies except with his
boots on, where no woman shuffled off the mortal coil
except in full dress, unless the jimjams claimed her as its
own. The society of Deadwood City, a mining town in a
district where the mines paid only imaginative dividends,
where the precious metal was always a little deeper down
in the mine, or in the side of a hill; where the water

19

washings amounted to just enough to pay current expenses, including carouses and "fun with the girls" as a part of such expenses, and to incite hope for a big find after a little while, was not of that character and description to yearn for. The demi-monde gave tone to all social gatherings, and the "gay gambler," who was the flushest, who sported the largest diamond pin, and who spent his money most freely, was the leading and most influential gentleman of the city. The woman who made the least secret about the color of her garters, and who was the "flyest of all the mob," was the belle of the place, the leader of the *ton,* the pet of society. To illustrate more fully the idea wished to be conveyed and to show the school wherein Sam Bass and his associates had taken a course, we will give extracts about Deadwood, published in metropolitan papers a short time after the Union Pacific Railroad robbery by Collins, Bass, and their confreres in crime. We will preface these extracts with the statement that Kitty LeRoy at one time lived in Dallas, Texas, doing jig dancing at Johnnie Thompson's Variety Theatre. She created somewhat of a furore in Dallas, not because of her beauty, for she was not what might be termed a remarkably pretty woman, but by the *naivete* of her manner, the personal magnetism that was peculiarly her own, and her charming, winning ways. But to the extracts. One letter-writer says: "Kitty LeRoy, who was killed by her husband only a short time ago, who then killed himself, was a small figure and had previously been noted as a jig dancer. She had a large Roman nose, cold grey eyes, a low cunning forehead, and was inordinately fond of money. I saw her often in her 'Mint,' which was opposite my office, where men congregated to squander their money, and as Kitty was a good player, like the old grave-digger, she 'gathered them in,' that is, their money. Men are, in a general sense, fools. A tress of golden hair, or a bright eye or soft cheek, will precipitate them into an ocean of folly, and women of the world (and some out of the world) know this fact, and play upon the weak string of men's hearts until all is gone—money, character, and even life. Kitty had seen much of human nature, entering upon her wild career at the age of ten. She was married three times and died at the age of twenty-eight. A polite and intelligent German met her. He was doing well with his gold claim; she knew it. Like the spider, she spun her delicate web about him until he poured into her lap $8,000 in gold, and then when his claim would yield no more she beat him over the head with a bottle and drove him from her door. One and another she married, and then when their money was gone, discarded them in rapid succession. Yet there was something peculiarly magnetic about Kitty. Men did love her, and there are men living today who love her memory. Well, she's gone. I saw her only a short time since lying dead by the inanimate body of her husband, with whom she would not live but with whom she was obliged to pass quietly to the grave." Still another correspondent writes of Deadwood society, and very sweetly of Kitty, speaks thusly: "There are dance-houses and theatres, where the gay society congregate, and it is at such houses, as well as at the gambling houses, that the fair sex may be seen. The women, though not so bad as the men, are all strong-minded, which from a henpecked point of view, is the worst thing you can say of a female. Some keep bars, taverns, boardinghouses and variety shows, while a few keep gambling dens, like the 'Mint,' kept by poor Kitty LeRoy, who was killed by one of her husbands, which was the tragic end of a brilliant career;

for, barring the wild, gypsy-like attire, which fashion would fail to appreciate as intensely picturesque, Kitty LeRoy was what a real man would call a starry beauty. Her brow was low, and her brown hair thick and curling; she had five husbands, seven revolvers, a dozen bowie-knives, and always went armed to the teeth, which latter were like pearls set in coral. She was a terrific gambler, and wore in her ears immense diamonds, which shone almost like her glorious eyes. The magnetism about her marvelous beauty was such as to drive her lovers crazy; more men had been killed about her than all the other women in the hills combined, and it was only a question whether her lovers or herself had killed the most. She could throw a bowie-knife straighter than any pistol bullet, except her own, and married her first husband because he was the only man of all her lovers who had the nerve to let her shoot an apple off his head while she rode by at full speed. On one occasion she disguised herself in male attire to fight a man who refused to combat with a woman. He fell, and she then cried, and married him in time to be his widow. Kitty was sometimes rich and sometimes poor, but always lavish as a prince when she had money. She dealt vantoon and faro, and played all games and cards with a dexterity that amounted to genius."

We have thus briefly sketched Deadwood society, so that the reader can form an idea of the school in which Bass and his confederates had graduated and prepared themselves for train robbers. Ogallala was the objective point on the Union Pacific road, several hundred miles away from Deadwood City, and to that point the gang hastened under the leadership of Joel Collins. The leader laid his plans well. They camped near the railroad station for about a week studying the situation and recruiting their horses. Collins came to the conclusion that Big Spring Station, several miles west of Ogallala, would be a better place for his purposes; they rode over there the morning of the night they accomplished their objects, reconnoitering and maturing their plans, and then went back into the woods, about half a mile away, and secured their horses in a secret place, and at night returned to the station. Here they took position on the platform, capturing the station agent and his assistant, they being the only men at the place. These they kept under guard. This was on the night of September 19, 1877. At ten o'clock the train drew up to the station to take on water. Collins and Heffridge, with cocked revolvers, captured the engineer and fireman, and marching them out to where Berry and Nixon had the station agent and his assistant under guard, turned them over to their custody. In the meantime Bass and Davis had secured the express messenger and were trying to force him to open the iron safe. He replied that he could not do it, that it was a time lock and no one could open it until it reached its destination. Davis ranted like an insane man, beat the messenger over the head and jabbed two or three teeth out of his mouth with the muzzle of his pistol, lacerating his lips. The messenger handed them a paper explaining the way to open the safe when the combination ran down, which Collins on reading stated to his men that the messenger was powerless to open the safe and to let him be. Bass then seized an axe and tried in vain to open it. There were $200,000 in gold in the safe. In one end of the car they found some silver bullion in bricks, but they being too heavy for them, they let them be. In rummaging through the car, Davis found some small boxes sealed with sealing wax, and breaking one open, twenty-dollar gold pieces rolled out. They

23

secured the contents of these boxes, $60,000 in twenty-dollar gold pieces. They went through the coaches robbing the passengers, and from them got $400 and several gold watches. Bass would make the passengers hold their hands up while Davis would systematically go through their pockets. One elderly man holding up only one hand, Bass cursed him and told him to hold up the other, when the old man showed him a stump of an arm, and replying that he had only one hand to hold up. Seeing this Sam gave him his money back, saying, "I don't want a one-armed man's money."

Having finished the job, the train was permitted to go on. They took their money and hid it in the sand on the bank of South Platte River, when they returned to Ogallala, where they remained two days. Finding that they were not suspected of the robbery, they divided their gold, each taking $10,000 and putting it in strong sacks, they separated, going in pairs. Bass and Davis went together, Collins and Heffridge, and Berry and Nixon, the two latter heading for Missouri, while the other four set out for Texas.

Bass and Davis had no adventures on their dreary ride over the plains, and when they got into Kansas they traded off one of their horses for a buggy and swapped the other one for a horse that would work, and in their buggy with the gold in the bottom of it they proceeded on their way to Texas. They camped one night in Kansas with a squad of soldiers who were hunting for them and who made inquiries about them. Had they been on horseback, they might have been suspicioned, but traveling as they were in an old buggy and representing themselves as farmers from Western Kansas going into the Eastern part of the state to look for work, their crops having failed, they were not molested or in any way interfered with. Continuing their journey, Bass and Davis reached Denton on November 1, 1877, the trip from the scene of the robbery occupying forty days.

Berry and Nixon after leaving Ogallala separated, Nixon going to Florida, and Berry to his home near Mexico, Missouri. Thinking himself safe at home, Berry was exceedingly imprudent in his conversation and actions. He boasted openly of having $10,000 in gold, which he claimed he had made mining in the Black Hills. Those who knew him doubted this because Berry had always been a thriftless "ne'er-do-well," and people began to suspect that he had had a hand in the Union Pacific robbery. He had been at home but a little while when he exchanged $9,000 in gold for currency, and the same day ordered a suit of clothes from a tailor. As the gold he exchanged was all of the coinage of 1877, and as the $60,000 taken from the express car was all of that coinage, suspicion of Berry's complicity in that robbery ripened into strong belief, and the officers determined to arrest him. A watch was kept on the tailor shop so as to catch him when he went to get his clothes. But he seems to have had an inkling of what was on foot and sent a friend for his clothes. This friend was followed by the officers to Berry's house, where the officers divided, a part remaining in front to watch the house and the others going around a small field to come up to the rear of the house. While this party was going through the woods, they heard a horse pawing the ground, and going towards the sound, they saw a horse bridled and saddled hitched to a tree. Close by the horse Berry was asleep on the ground. They waked him up and ordered him to surrender. His reply was a pistol shot, which being returned by the posse, he fell mortally wounded. He was taken to the house, where he lived two or three days, and in his last hours told all about the Big Springs robbery and who was in it.

The robbery had created the wildest excitement, especially among the railroad and express officials. They knew that it would be a difficult and expensive undertaking to guard all trains through the long, uninhabited waste through which they passed on the plains, and they knew that every road agent in the West, when they heard of the large amount of money that had been bagged by the robbers, would be tempted to try it, so the railroad and express people determined to capture the robbers, if possible. They offered large rewards for their capture and induced the State of Nebraska also to offer a large reward. This put the detectives and officers upon the *qui vive* all over the country.

It was not at first known who any of the robbers were and there was no clue to go by, but it happened that a young man named Andy Riley was on the train the night it was robbed, and standing upon the platform of one of the coaches, he recognized Joel Collins. He had traveled with Collins to Deadwood, and had seen him and talked to him a few days before the robbery, at Ogallala. As soon as he reached Omaha, he notified the officials, and then there was a clue to the perpetrators. The names of Collins and his men, for they had become well known while they stayed at Ogallala, and a full description of them, were telegraphed in every direction. It was learned, too, that the robbers crossed the Platte River, in Nebraska, and that on the 23d of September, four days after the robbery, they were at Young's ranch on the Republican River. We have given an account of the courses pursued by all the robbers except Collins and his companion Heffridge; and we will follow them up to the last chapter of the drama.

The First Big Steal

Sheriff Bardsley, of Ellis County, Kansas, had been put in possession of all the facts of the robbery, and a description of the men. He knew from the information he had that they were coming towards Kansas, and he determined to keep a look-out for them. To this end he started for Hays City, on the Kansas and Pacific Railroad, with a trained detective and ten United States cavalrymen, under the command of Lieutenant Allen. Sixty miles west of Hays City is Buffalo Station, and there Sheriff Bardsley established his headquarters, going into camp in a ravine out of sight of the station. He did this because the station was in the midst of a wild, dreary waste, uninhabited, and he judged the robbers would be more likely to pass that way, than any other. On the morning of the 26th of September, two horsemen driving a pack pony were seen coming up to the station. No particular attention was paid to them by Sheriff Bardsley, for he was looking for six men, not two. Had they gone by, they never would have been suspected or molested. But they did not do this. Fate seemed to have ordained that a speedy retribution should overtake them for their crime. There is no evil ever committed that is not followed by punishment. The two men, who were Collins and Heffridge, stopped behind the station house, Heffridge remaining with the horses while Collins went to the station agent and inquired the way to Thompson's Store. Being directed, he went there, and made some purchases. While he was talking to the station agent, however, he pulled out his handkerchief and left exposed in his pocket a letter, on which the superscription "Joel Collins" was plainly visible to the agent standing by. In answer to inquiries, Heffridge, who was with the horses, said they were Texas cattle men on their way home, and he inquired the way to Fort Larned. The agent at

27

once notified Sheriff Bardsley, and he came up to the station from his camp and engaged in conversation with Collins. They talked together some time, taking a drink of whisky at the station-house. Collins did not conceal his name, for he had no idea that it could be known at that little way-station that he was engaged in the Big Springs robbery. After awhile Collins and Heffridge started on their journey, and directly Bardsley and his cavalrymen started in pursuit, soon overtaking them, for they made no effort to escape. Sheriff Bardsley, on halting them, said: "I have a description of some train robbers which answers well to your appearance. I want you and your partner to return with me to the station. You need fear nothing if you are innocent, and if you are the men I want, then I am $10,000 better off. Please come back to the station, gentlemen." Collins replied: "You are mistaken in your men, gentlemen," laughing as he spoke, "but of course there is no use to object. We will go back and have the mistake explained. We are Texas boys going home, that's all." They then turned their horses about, exchanging a few low words, and started back with the posse towards the station. After riding a few hundred yards, Collins exclaimed: "Pard, if we have to die, we might as well die game," and instantly both men drew their revolvers, but before they could fire, they were riddled with bullets by the posse and fell from their horses dead. Thus went out in infamy and shame two young lives because of their crime and their evil ways. On the pack-pony was found, in an old pair of pantaloons, $25,000 in $20 gold pieces of the coinage of 1877. Collins' friends have always claimed that he was not in the Big Springs train robbery, but that he was murdered for his money, money made in stock speculations in Idaho and Nebraska, but there is no doubt of his guilt, Berry and Bass both having stated, on their dying beds, that he was the leader of the gang. When the bodies of Collins and his companions were taken to the station, a number of Texans recognized Collins, and a woman declared his companion to be William Cotts, formerly of Pottsville, Pennsylvania, but more recently of San Antonio, Texas. Cotts may have been his name, but he was known with the gang as Bill Heffridge.

CHAPTER V

The Texas Gang Formed

Bass and Davis separate—Jackson and Underwood enlist
under Captain Sam Bass—A rollicking bout in
San Antonio—Capture and escape of Under-
wood, suspicioned of being Nixon

BASS AND Davis did not stop in Denton County, but passing through went on to Fort Worth, where they separated, Davis going to New Orleans. Bass went to Cooke County from Fort Worth, and pitched camp in Cave Hollow, near the cattle ranche of Bob Murphy, not far from Rosston. He visited Denton, not long after his return, waiting until after night-fall to do so. There he sought an interview with Frank Jackson, who with his brother-in-law, Key, was engaged in working at the tinner's trade at that place. As soon as he was able to see Jackson, he began to persuade and insist upon him to go with him. He had $10,000 (ten thousand dollars) in gold in his belt, which he poured into his hat, at the same time saying: "Now just lay down them tinner's tools and go with me and I'll insure that you get plenty of this." Frank was slow to accept the inducements held out to him, and Bass jerked up a handful of $20 gold pieces and said, "Here, I'll give you this. I've got plenty of it, and if you will go with me I'll insure you get $100 a month. We may have a little racket now and then, but I've never had any trouble yet, and there's not much danger." But Jackson was not yet to be won by such golden promises; he still resisted on his second interview with Bass, nor did he yield until the latter had visited him the third time, on which occasion he allowed himself to be persuaded, and gave his promise to go. Though it was not generally known that Bass was a participator in the Big Springs robbery, at least at that time, yet he was very secret and stealthy in his movements, and always made his visits to the city after dark, and was very careful to excite as little attention as possible. But in the country he threw aside caution, and circulated freely and boldly among his old acquaintances. He told Jim Murphy that he had been in the Black Hills where he had located some mines, and had struck several rich leads which he had been very successful in disposing of. To use his own expression, he had sold out for "big money"; that he had also had splendid luck in his racing ventures, that he was in funds. About the middle of November he purchased a couple of horses from Murphy, when he was at once joined by Frank Jackson and Henry Underwood, and the three started out to San Antonio. They were pursued by Everheart, sheriff of Grayson County, and Tom Gerren, deputy sheriff of Denton County, they having been apprised of the rewards offered for Bass by the Express Company. Unfortunately these officers did not agree, and accused each other of every imaginable crime. Bass afterward stated that he and his party were in San Antonio on a general carousal; that they were enjoying themselves immensely and having what is called a general "good time"; that he knew nothing about the two officers being after them; that he had never seen either of them, though Jackson had one day met Gerren on the street, and that they did not leave San Antonio on account of the officers. It has been stated by

31

Gerren that while there he one day saw Bass on one of the streets of San Antonio, and that if it had not been for Everheart's interference he would have shot him then and there, as he had already raised his gun to his shoulder for that purpose when Everheart prevented him, consequently they lost their prey, for the party getting hint of their presence and intentions toward themselves, immediately, and without ceremony, decamped for "pastures new." Finding that they were pursued, Bass and his gang began to take measures to elude, or mislead, their enemies, the emissaries of the law, and so turned back into the edge of Cooke County, and camped at a place overgrown with brush, which was almost inaccessible, called Cave Hollow, a canyon of Clear Creek. They were still pursued by Everheart, who, with his posse, invested Underwood's house, it having been alleged that Underwood was really Tom Nixon, and Pinkerton's detectives having been employed to arrest him as Nixon. During the night of December 24, 1877, Underwood visited his family, and remained with them all night. The following morning Everheart caused the house to be surrounded, and ordered Underwood to surrender, informing him that as Tom Nixon, he had orders from the proper authorities to arrest him. Of course Underwood assured him that his name was not Nixon, and, also, that he did not propose to surrender. However, upon Everheart's telling him that every man in his posse would swear to his being one of the Big Springs train robbers, and that his name was Nixon, Underwood seeing that there was no possible way of escape, finally surrendered, and was taken to Kearney, Nebraska, and, as Tom Nixon, was lodged in jail at that place. The reward for Nixon, of $500, it is said, was paid on the apprehension of Underwood. Underwood, it may be stated here, at the date of the Big Springs robbery, September 18, 1877, was in Denton County, and had never been suspected of having anything to do with a robbery of any kind. He could have proved an *alibi* by any number of the best citizens, without trouble, consequently, a wrong was committed when he was arrested and carried to Nebraska, in Nixon's place, for, however bad a man he may have been, it was scant justice to punish him in this way without giving him a shadow of a chance to prove his innocence of the charge brought against him.

Here, in the Kearney jail, he was kept in close confinement until he made his escape therefrom, April, 1878. During the period of his confinement in the jail he made the acquaintance of "Arkansaw Johnson," whose real name was Huckston. The wife of this man managed to convey to them a number of steel saws, concealed in a bucket of butter. This bucket being furnished with a false bottom, the saws were placed under it, and the butter put on the bottom. He also obtained a steel spring, or shank, which he converted into a saw, from the sole of an old shoe which had been thrown into the passway around the cell, and it being kicked near his cell by persons passing, he obtained possession of it, and converted it, by his ingenuity, into a useful instrument to help him to escape from captivity. He also obtained from a fellow prisoner, who had only been confined a short time for some small offense, an additional supply of saws, and a bottle of nitric acid, with which to soften the steel bars of his cage. And with the aid of all these instruments, it took him three weeks to cut his way out—three weeks of hard, steady work. His mode of operation was the following: In the first place, on the wall, which was plastered, there was a

33

paper containing the rules of the jail, which he raised, it being only tacked, and cut into the plaster a hole as a repository for his various implements, when not at work with them; here they were placed and the paper neatly tacked over them, completely concealing them from all curious or prying eyes. In cutting the bars, he used the acid and the saws, and when he left off work, filling the cuts with a dark-colored soap, which effectually concealed them also. At length having made a breach large enough, he effected his escape during the night. Enclosing the jail was a fence made of barbed wire, and upon encountering this, Underwood put his foot upon one wire, and pulled up the next with his hands, thus forming an opening. Arkansaw escaped between his legs, through the opening, and thus opened the way in a similar manner for Underwood. They then made their way to the stables of a judge, who lived in the suburbs, and was owner of some excellent horses, Arkansaw piloting the way, as being familiar with the locality as well as the facts of the case, where they stole two of the best animals, with their proper equipments, and started out for Texas. When they set out it was about two o'clock, and a cold, dark, and dismal night, and as they were but thinly and scantily clad, they felt the cold severely. But despite scanty clothing, freezing darkness, and want of money—for they had but fifty cents between them—they persevered and pushed ahead, for freedom is sweet to all, and though the price to be paid for liberty be dear, the love of it is implanted in every heart, and it is man's nature to make any sacrifice to attain it, to risk anything and everything—even life itself to that end. So, in spite of the risk they ran of freezing to death, they pushed on, only stimulated and saved from such a death by the excitement of the hour, and the hope that

34

cheered them of escaping at last. According to Henry Underwood's statement, and the account is taken from him, they made the trip through to Denton County, Texas, in seventeen days, not missing a single meal on the way, neither they nor their horses. On one occasion in Kansas, they made a raid on an old lady's larder, and were rewarded by the sight of a beautifully dressed and cooked turkey gobbler, which they appropriated and made off with on the principle that "might makes right" —especially for a hungry man—or two hungry men— and which they had the satisfaction of feasting off of for several days. As their fifty cents went for whisky at the first cross-roads grocery they came to, it naturally followed that they begged and stole their way through.

CHAPTER VI

Allen Station

*Stage robbing—The inception of the
train robberies in Texas*

W HEN SAM BASS returned to Cove Hollow from San
Antonio, on or about the 20th of December, 1877,
he and his gang conceived and matured the plan of
robbing the stage running from Fort Worth to Cleburne,
Texas. About ten miles from Fort Worth they took their
stations on the road side, to await the coming of the stage,
which late in the evening reached that point, bearing only
two passengers. They covered the surprised driver with
their guns, and commanded him to throw up his "props,"
which order he promptly obeyed. They then gave their
attention to the passengers, who were called to come forth
and throw up their hands, while Bass examined the
condition of their finances. Sam Bass quietly and coolly
proceeded to rifle the pockets of his victims, while the
others kept them covered with their guns, but the result
was not very satisfactory, being only eleven dollars. After
some grumbling and complaining among the gang as to
the lean and meagre condition of the pockets, from which
they had hoped for so much richer a harvest, and giving
it as their opinion that there should be a law to prohibit
the traveling of such poor trash, the hack was allowed to
proceed on its way, its luckless inmates being as much

dissatisfied as Mr. Sam Bass and his lawless gang. The band proceeded to Fort Worth from this place, passed the night there, then wended their way to Cove Hollow. Here Underwood was arrested on the 24th. After this Bass and Jackson went below Denton, to a thickly wooded region near Green Hills, among the breaks of Hickory Creek, where they could, without difficulty, hide from any number of pursuers. While staying here, they took little or no pains to conceal themselves from the country people among whom they had many friends and acquaintances, who were willing to harbor them in case of emergency. After some weeks they grew tired of so tame a life, and thought they would try another stage robbery. After looking around, they selected a spot between Marysville and Fort Worth. Concealing their horses in a thicket hard by, they masked themselves and awaited the coming of the stage. In due time it came, having aboard three passengers, and as usual Bass searched them—they seeing the guns aimed at them, offered no resistance—getting this time about $70.00 in money and three valuable watches. They then returned to Denton County, and from there to their old camping grounds, in Cove Hollow, in Cooke County, greatly encouraged and very jubilant over their recent success.

From this time dates a series of the most daring train robberies that were ever placed upon record—a disgrace to this country or any other. The deeds of Jack Sheppard and other highwaymen who used to entrap unwary travelers upon the King's highway, are utterly tame and insignificant when compared to these high-handed robbers, who coolly step upon the iron track, stop the snorting "iron-horse of commerce," plunder express and mail trains, while the officers of same stand powerless before the muzzles of cocked revolvers and guns, and the terrified passengers sit shivering and helpless before the lawless and well-armed gang. Never in the annals of history have been recorded such audacious, cool, and deliberate proceedings as the Texas robberies. They kept it up even after it was known that the officers on every train were on their guard, and that the express and mail trains contained heavily armed men.

The first robbery of this kind was committed at Allen Station, a small place six miles north of McKinney, on the Houston and Texas Central Railroad, and twenty-four miles north of Dallas, on the night of February 22nd. The south-bound train was immediately boarded, when it reached the station, by four men, all masked; one of them jumped upon the engine, and menaced the engineer and fireman with a cocked revolver. The remaining robbers made a rush for the express car, and tried to force their way in, but Mr. J. L. A. Thomas—the messenger— gallantly repulsed them. Mr. Thomas was standing at the door of the car when the train stopped, and the robbers cried out to him, "Throw up your hands; your money or your brains." Whereupon he jumped back into the car, and got his pistol ready. The robbers began firing, which fire he returned, discharging his revolver several times. They sprang into the car, the bellrope was cut, the express car uncoupled from the rest of the train, and Thomas was ordered to surrender, telling him that if he did not, they would set fire to it. The engineer was also ordered to draw it over the switch. They then began the task of rifling the safe of its contents. At this time, the amount they secured was said to be $2,500; it was subsequently learned to be nearly $3,000.

The passengers, of whom there was a large number

38

aboard, evidently considered discretion the better part of
valor, for they took no measures whatever against defending themselves, but hastily concealed whatever valuables
they possessed about their persons, or any other available
place, every moment expecting the robbers to come
through the train and demand what they had. But
wonderful to relate, as soon as they had finished rifling
the express car, they departed, moving in a westerly
direction. Although Texas had witnessed many robberies
and crimes of all kinds, this bold and daring deed caused
much excitement in every quarter. Still the efforts made
to capture the robbers were rather feeble, except those
made by the Express Company—the chief sufferers. They
at once instituted a vigorous search, and by their means
Tom Spotswood was arrested at his cattle ranche, on
Little Elm Creek, Denton County, on February 27th.
Mr. W. K. Cornish, express agent at Dallas, and Mr.
Thomas, the messenger, were leaders of the party that
effected this arrest. They took Spotswood to McKinney,
where, after a preliminary examination, and in default of
bail ($2,500), he was carried to jail, there to await his
trial at the next term of the District Court.

In the trial that ensued Mr. Thomas was the principal
witness. His testimony was, that among the men who
entered the car on the night of the robbery, one was not
masked, and in him he recognized the person of Tom
Spotswood; that he had plenty of time to recognize the
prisoner, for he held a cocked revolver directly in his face,
while another man robbed the safe. He furthermore
noticed a peculiarity about him, namely: his glass eye.
His evidence had great weight with the jury, although
some have raised the question as to how straight a man
can see with a cocked revolver held in his face. It would

undoubtedly take a man of nerve, and that Thomas proved himself to be. The trial lasted from the latter part of June until July 2d.

A saloon-keeper at Allen Station, a Mr. Newman, testified that on the day before the robbery Spotswood came into his saloon, and, among other questions, asked if there was any gaming carried on in town, saying that he was a sporting man himself, and inquiring as to what time the train came in from the north. Some of his friends made an attempt to prove an *alibi*. The brother of the prisoner, Bill Spotswood, and another man, swore that Tom slept at the house of the former on the night in question, but this was contradicted by two other witnesses, who testified to having seen Bill Spotswood and his companion as they were chopping wood in a woods near by, the next morning, and they said they had not slept at home the night before on account of not being able to get across the creek. A verdict of guilty was returned by the jury, and he was sentenced to ten years in the penitentiary.

Spotswood was granted a new trial on the ground of newly discovered evidence, and through the law's delays, worked by able and learned counsel, he staved off a second hearing of his case until the spring term of the Collin County District Court, when, by shrewd and skillful management, he obtained a verdict of not guilty. Under a wise provision of the law, every person charged with an offense against the law is presumed to be innocent until guilt is proven, and, of course, this legal provision has binding force and effect after acquittal. Being declared innocent by a tribunal of legal jurisdiction, no one has a right to say that Tom Spotswood was a participant in the Allen Station train robbery. It is morally certain, however, that if he had been tried in the United States courts, as were the other prisoners captured, he would not so easily have secured his acquittal. This is not said because a defendant in a federal court in Texas does not have a fair trial, for such is not the case, but because the federal courts are not hampered with the legal technicalities and special requirements of which skillful criminal lawyers avail themselves in the state courts to aid their clients out of difficulties. The Code of Criminal Procedure in vogue in Texas is but a tissue of mere technicalities, all of which tend to defeat justice, and force society, and not the criminal, to run the gauntlet on every criminal trial. The penal laws themselves, of Texas, are of remarkable excellence, but handicapped as they are with the Code of Criminal Procedure under and in accordance with which all persons charged with offenses against the state must be tried, they are well nigh rendered nugatory, well nigh dead letters on the statute book.

Spotswood was not arraigned for trial in the United States court, for the reason that the mails were not molested at the Allen Station robbery, and if he was *particeps criminus* in that robbery he had violated no federal law.

CHAPTER VII

Two More Trains Stopped

*Hutchins and Eagle Ford made to figure in history —
Little money but two men shot — The thing
is becoming monotonous*

THE EXCITEMENT of the Allen Station train robbery had
scarcely died out in North Texas before the people of
the country were startled with the announcement that
the Houston and Texas Central express train had been
robbed again. This time it proved to be at Hutchins, a
little way-station in Dallas County, ten miles south of the
city of Dallas.

Hutchins is a small hamlet, containing twenty-five
houses, including two or three stores, and exclusive of the
railroad depot buildings, two in number. The south-bound
express train passed that point at ten o'clock at night, and
as in quiet little country villages like Hutchins, everybody
goes to bed early. There was no one up in fact, except the
station agent and a Negro, and the work of the robbers
was easy so far as molestation from outside sources was
concerned.

The night of the 18th of March was an exceedingly
dark one, just suited in its blackness to aid such nefarious
work as that soon to be perpetrated. The robbers, three
in number, Bass, Jackson, and Barnes, rode up to the
station a little while before train time, and making

prisoners of the agent and a Negro who was with him to assist him in his labors about the depot, they waited patiently for the approach of the train, the glare of the headlight of which was then visible a mile away. On sped the train, not a soul on board dreaming of danger or molestation ahead. In the sleeping car some passengers had gone to bed and others were chatting pleasantly; in the other coaches the passengers were smoking or reading, as best they could by the struggling lights to be found on railroad trains, the express messenger was busy getting his Hutchins freight ready for delivery, and the route agent, alone in all his dignity of privacy in his mail car, was sorting his letters and paper packages and making up his pouches for wayside delivery. No one was dreaming of train robbers; no one expected the scene in a few moments to be enacted.

As the train drew up to the station and before it had stopped its motion, Frank Jackson had jumped aboard the tender and with presented pistol made the engineer and fireman hold up their hands and stop the train. When asked by the engineer what he wanted, he answered, "We want money, that's all, and there's no use kicking." The reply to which was, Jackson afterwards said, "All right, go ahead, it's no skin off our backs." Bass and Barnes captured also two tramp printers who were stealing a ride on the pilot of the engine. These two men, with the station agent and Negro, they marched in front of them, in their attack upon the express car, so that if the messenger should make resistance, they would be a breastwork between them and his fire, though they really believed that if they had the station agent and these three other men in front of them the messenger would not fire upon them for fear of killing one of them. The express messenger, hearing the unusual commotion and seeing armed men approaching his car, shut and barred the door and put himself upon the defensive, after extinguishing his lights. The robbers were not to be baffled in this way. They were too near to their prize to give it up without a master effort, and they soon burst the car door in and were received by a shot from the messenger, Thomas (who is a brother to the messenger robbed at Allen Station), which they returned. He kept up his fire with his pistol until he had discharged every barrel but one, and as he could not reach his cartridges to reload, and had been severely wounded in the face, he surrendered. During the firing one of the printers, Bennet by name, was wounded in the calf of the leg, a perfect godsend to him, for it secured him a comfortable bed, plenty of rations, and toddies in abundance free of charge. He convalesced very slowly and required a free administration of stimulants. He fared sumptuously, and his fare was so much better than hand-outs that he was loth to get well at all. His wound healed entirely too fast to suit him.

There are different statements as to the amount of money stolen from the express car. They could have obtained from the passengers a quantity of jewelry but did not desire to be encumbered with it. Had they looked in the stove they would have found a large amount of money and valuables secreted by Messenger Thomas after he extinguished his lights.

After finishing the express car, the light-fingered gentry paid their respects to the route agent, and went through his mails as adroitly as if they had been in the postal service all their lives. They got little money in the postal car, for checks and post office orders were of no value to them. Had Bass and his men not been so ignorant, they never would have molested the mails. They never got over

$25 in money by any mail robbery they committed—bank checks and post office money orders being useless to them—and they brought down the ire of the federal government, that never lets up when it starts after an offender, upon themselves, the consequences of which Sam Pipes and Albert Herndon are now serving life terms in prison.

In this robbery the passengers on the train were permitted to go, as there were only three robbers in the party, and they had been so delayed in robbing the express, and the pistol firing had been so heavy, the citizens of the place might be aroused and come to the rescue of the train. After finishing their job, the train pursued its way, and the robbers left Hutchins hurriedly, going in a northwest direction, toward the Trinity River bottom, only a few miles distant.

Messenger Thomas gave up his route at Corsicana on account of his wound, which was a painful one, laying him up some weeks. For his gallantry in defending his car and his foresight in secreting the bulk of the money in his charge, Messenger Thomas was suitably rewarded by the Express Company.

The station agent, who was also telegraph operator at Hutchins, flashed the news of the robbery all over the country as soon as he was released from arrest, giving as accurate a description of the robbers, who were masked, and their horses, as he could. Intelligence of the outlawry reached Dallas about 11 o'clock, and as soon as W. F. Morton, the city marshal, heard it, he organized a small party and started at once to try to intercept the robbers. He went direct to Hutchins, and getting what information he could there, proceeded at once on the hunt, riding thirty-five miles, including the ride to Hutchins, before sun-up the next morning. But all pursuit was in vain. There was no clue to the perpetrators of the deed, and it had been so long dry that it was impossible to follow their trail, consequently it was mere groping in the dark, and active search for them was soon abandoned.

This second robbery, so bold and daring in all its details, began to arouse the people. The railroad and express companies became uneasy; people almost got afraid to travel. Northern and Western newspapers, of a certain class, those who never see anything good in the South, especially Texas, began to talk about the extreme lawlessness in Texas, and the inefficiency of the officers of the law, when passenger trains could be stopped and robbed and the United States mails rifled with impunity in two of the most populous counties in the state. Not only were the state authorities aroused to the necessity of action, but federal officials too began to prepare for action. The hand of outlawry had been raised against the United States, and that too, in a Southern state, which made it only the worse, for, of course, it was only an offshoot of rebellion. The Express Company hired a guard to go with the messenger on every train on both the Houston and Texas Central and on the Texas and Pacific roads, because they did not know when and where another blow might be struck. It was not long before it came.

A few days before the Hutchins robbery took place, Bass, Jackson, and Barnes, in their camp in Denton County, discussed the practicability of robbing the train at Hutchins. Barnes was sick and unable for duty, so Bass and Jackson rode down to Hutchins to reconnoitre and see how the land lay. They ascertained the hour the train going south arrived at the station, and studied closely all the difficulties they would encounter, and were

46

seriously inclined themselves to make the venture of the robbery, but on reflection, concluded to return to camp and await Barnes' convalescence, having to wait only a few days.

CHAPTER VIII

Eagle Ford

The Texas-Pacific Road comes in for a share of the fun—
A recruit in the ranks of Captain Bass does
service—The slimmest haul of all—The
express car guarded but no fight made

THE ROBBERY of the train at Hutchins was on the night of the 18th of March, 1878, and just seventeen days afterward, on the night of April 4th, a Texas and Pacific west-bound train was tackled and made to yield up its bounty.

About the latter part of March, Henry Underwood, in company with "Arkansaw" Johnson, having escaped from the Nebraska jail where he was confined on suspicion of being Nixon, one of the Union Pacific train robbers, arrived in Denton County, where his family was, and proceeded, he and Johnson, to join Bass. Billy Wetzel, a deputy sheriff of Denton County, was in Bass's camp playing poker with the boys when Jim Murphy told Bass that Underwood had arrived at home. This put Bass in a great glee, and he immediately left the camp and proceeded to Underwood's house, returning without him late in the evening. Wetzel remained all night with the bandits, playing poker with them, and while he was there, Billy Scott, of Dallas, and Billie Collins, of Dallas County, a

48

brother of Joel Collins, came into camp. The next day Underwood and Johnson came to the camp, and Wetzel having a capias for Underwood, read it to him and gave him a blank bond to fill, which he consented to at once, but by persuasion of Bass he declined afterwards to do it until after a few days.

Time hung heavily upon the hands of Bass, and he proposed to rob the Texas and Pacific train at Eagle Ford. In the meantime Frank Jackson had seen some of his relatives, living in Denton County, and under their persuasions and tears, he had about made up his mind to quit Bass and change his mode of life. His better instincts and nature had been aroused and he realized how rapidly he was going down the hill of ruin to sure punishment and degradation, therefore he declined to go on the Eagle Ford expedition. Barnes was sick and could not go, and Underwood, having just returned home from prison, desired to stay with his family, so neither of these three men were concerned in the robbery only as accessories before and after the fact. Bass thought it would be a good idea for them to remain behind anyhow because he had been made aware that some suspicion was pointing to him and his confreres, as probable participants in the Allen Station and Hutchins robberies, and if Jackson, and Underwood and Barnes were known to be in Denton County, in their accustomed pursuits of gambling, drinking, and riding around when a train at Eagle Ford was robbed, why it would divert suspicion from him and his confederates. He wanted to try Arkansaw Johnson's mettle, and he concluded that he and Johnson and "two novices" in Dallas County he knew of, who were anxious to know how it was done, would do the work.

Eagle Ford is in Dallas County, and as the west-bound

express train arrived at that station at 11 o'clock on the night of April 4th, it was boarded by Bass and his squad and easily captured. He and party hid themselves under the platform, and as the train approached, they captured the station agent, and when the cars had stopped, took the engineer and fireman in charge and then marched upon the express car, carrying out the usual tactics of marching the prisoners in front of them as a breastwork. The express car was closed and bolted and Bass made the station agent ask the messenger to open it. This he refused to do, so Bass burst it open with a stick of wood. The robbers then entered it and plundered it of what they could find of value to them and then proceeded to pilfer the mails. Only $50 in money was obtained from the express car, and a few registered letters from the mail car. In the express car were Mr. Hickox armed with a shot gun, and a hired guard with a shot gun and six-shooter, but neither of them offered any resistance. Strange, indeed, is it not that four masked men could coolly and deliberately rob a train in the presence of fifty or sixty passengers, the train employes, a United States postal route agent, and express messenger and guard, with perfect impunity, no hand being raised to stop them. Yet such was the case at Eagle Ford.

After the robbery, the two country amateurs received their portion of the spoil, according to Bass's own account, and repaired to their homes thoroughly cured of the train robbing business, utterly demoralized by their first act of lawlessness of so heinous a nature, wiser and forever after, honester and better men, it is sincerely to be hoped. Who these two country men of Dallas County were has never transpired, and never will, in all probability. Sam Bass and "Arkansaw" Johnson were the only two men who could have told, and they are both dead, and both died carrying the secret with them. It was contended by the train men that there were five men in this robbery, but Sam Bass always said there were but four. If there were five, the fifth man was Seaborn Barnes. As there could have been no motive in Bass misrepresenting the matter, the fifth man seen by the train men, must have been a man in Buckram.

Bass and "Arkansaw" Johnson did not return to Denton County immediately after the Eagle Ford robbery, according to his statement, but spent several days in Dallas County, enjoying themselves with friends.

This third robbery, each one following so fast on the heels of the other, created intense excitement. People began to wonder who was safe. The air was filled with rumors, and dread of raids upon the towns began to agitate the public mind. Frantic appeals were made to the state government for protection, and the officers of the law were soundly berated in the newspapers and on the street corners for not apprehending the perpetrators of the deeds. Yet no affidavit had ever been made charging anyone with committing the robberies, except against Tom Spotswood, who was in jail, and no warrants or capiases had been put into the hands of any officer. No one knew who the guilty parties were, though suspicion had begun to point towards Sam Bass and his gang, who were known to be in Denton County, and the people and officers of Denton County became the subjects of uncomplimentary remarks and jeers.

THE MESQUITE TRAIN ROBBERY

CHAPTER IX

Mesquite

The last train robbery—A gamey fight and several persons
wounded—A small amount of money obtained but
a hornet's nest raised—Brave Conductor
Alvord does his whole duty—The state
and federal authorities aroused

HAVING MADE arrangements in Dallas County for help whenever he needed it, and a place of rendezvous with the Collins boys, on Duck Creek, Bass and "Arkansaw" Johnson returned to their fastness in Denton County. In a few days Bass began to plan another robbery. He knew that excitement was running high and that suspicion was pointing towards him and the men who associated with him, but with daring bravado and fool-hardiness he determined to stop another train. The profits of the Allen Station, Hutchins, and Eagle Ford robberies had been small and he was not content to stop on such meagre pickings. He had had just such luck in robbing stage coaches in the Black Hills in Idaho Territory, but perseverance in his dangerous and nefarious occupation had resulted in a $10,000 haul at Big Springs, and he believed that luck would come to him again if he only kept on trying. He did not care for the danger, in fact he rather liked it, for it added zest to the life he was leading and gave him excitement. He was aware, too, that the cattle traders in Fort Worth were receiving now and then by express large sums of money to pay for cattle, and he thought that if he could just strike a train with a heavy remittance aboard, he could secure booty enough for himself and followers to justify them in changing their base of operations and entering upon pastures new, and he was bent on one more trial anyhow.

Having matured his plans and settled upon Mesquite Station on the Texas and Pacific Railway in Dallas County, and twelve miles east of Dallas, he and party consisting of Underwood, Jackson, Johnson, and Barnes, five in all, and known as the "regulars," proceeded to Dallas County, making the residence of William Collins their headquarters. They arrived at Collins' house on Monday night, April 8th, where they were joined by Sam Pipes and Albert G. Herndon, two young men about whom we will have more to say in another chapter. William Scott, who was playing the role of detective, and who had been in Bass's camp several times, also met them at Collins' house, though it seems that Scott was not aware of the fact that they were to be there, and had gone to Collins' house to get information as to when the next business was to come off. In other chapters a full account of Scott's work as detective and Collins' connection with the band will be given.

The gang discussed the situation while at Collins' house and Bass disclosed his plan of robbing the train at Mesquite. On Tuesday the 9th, William Collins, generally known as Billie, rode over to Mesquite, but a few miles from his residence, and took observations of how the land lay, and returning home, reported everything clear. That night the party rode over to the station to rob the train, but reaching there after train time, supposed they were

54

too late (though in reality they were not, for the train was behind time), and returned to Collins' house. Here they remained under cover all day.

Wednesday night, the 10th of April, 1878, they again went over to Mesquite Station, Bass, Underwood, Jackson, and Johnson, "the regulars," and Sam Pipes, Albert Herndon, and William Collins as "volunteers." Bass always said Will Scott was with the party in this robbery acting as an outside picket, but this is not generally believed, for the reason that, according to Bass's own account, and the account of others, Bass objected to so many "volunteers" going along, on the ground that too large a body would be unwieldy and the share of each in the booty would be made too small, which gave Scott, the detective, an opportunity to keep away.

Well, to resume, the party arrived at the station after dark, just before train time, which was 11 o'clock, and took positions behind the depot building, leaving their horses under charge of Billie Collins, and perhaps one other of the gang. As the train stopped, the station agent, Mr. Zurn, stepped out of his office on the platform with a paper to hand to the conductor, when he was confronted by one of the robbers with drawn pistol, and the remark, "Hold up your hands!" Taking in the situation at once, Mr. Zurn complied and surrendered a prisoner. Mrs. Zurn, the agent's wife, stepped out of her room in the depot building at this time, and was also ordered to hold up her hands, but paying no heed to the command, she turned and went back into her room followed with a volley of pistol balls from some of the miscreants as she fastened the door, none of which, fortunately, struck the lady. In the meantime Frank Jackson had captured the engineer, the fireman escaping and hiding under the platform. Mr. D. J. Healy, night clerk and telegraph operator at the Windsor Hotel in Dallas had been down to Terrell, and was returning home, and stepped off the train, while it was still in motion, to see and shake hands with his friend Zurn, operator and station agent at Mesquite, but he barely got on to the platform before a cocked revolver was thrust into his face with the command, "Follow me." Healy knew in a minute it was another train robbery, but he was very slow for all that in obeying the command, although he kept his hands up. About that time the train seemed to be starting off and his captor left him on a run toward the locomotive, crying out, "Stop it, don't let it get away." During that time Healy took occasion to hide in his boot $100 he had in his pocket, and as he straightened up his captor returned, ordering him again to follow, but as he walked too slowly to suit, another robber struck him on the back of the head with a pistol, stunning him slightly. Turning to the man who struck him, he denounced him as a coward, but at that instant both the robbers had their attention diverted by the firing on the train, and Healy availed himself of the opportunity to run, but not without being fired upon, the bullet going through his hat and knocking it off. There was some two hundred yards away a convict train, having on board a large number of convicts, working on the Texas-Pacific road, with a guard of sixteen men over them, and Healy ran to that train and took refuge with the guard. In the meantime Conductor Jules Alvord, who was in the sleeper when the train came up to Mesquite, stepped out on the platform of the sleeper to get out on the ground and attend to his duties at the station. He took in the situation at a glance, and although he had a small Derringer in his pocket, he went forward to another car and got a large six-shooter he had, and returning to the rear opened fire on the robbers. At his first shot he saw one of the miscreants sink back and go to the rear, as though he was wounded. The robbers promptly returned his fire, but he stood at his post, giving shot for shot. About his third shot he was wounded in the left arm, the bone being shattered and the flesh badly torn as though a heavy bullet had struck him. He then got down under the car and kept up his fire until his pistol was emptied, when his arm pained him so badly he entered the sleeper and bandaging up his arm laid down. A gentleman in the sleeper was dressing when he went in and told him he had a pistol and asked if he should go out and take a hand in the fun, but Conductor Alvord told him no, to remain in the sleeper and if the robbers came in there, to shoot them. When Conductor Alvord was exchanging shots with the robbers, one of them remarked to him, "You are a brave little cuss, but you are my meat." Another one said, "He is a game fellow and it's a pity to kill him."

In the meantime there were lively times ahead around the express car. Bass had demanded the opening of the door and the surrender of the parties within. The reply of the gallant Spofford Curley, the messenger, and his guard, Finellen, was a six-shooter bullet from Curley's pistol and a load of buck-shot from Finellen's shot-gun. Bass then procured a can of kerosene oil and smearing the car steps and sides with it, informed Curley that if he did not open the door, he would set fire to the car and either burn him and the guard up or kill them as they left the car, and that if by the time he had counted fifty the door was not open he would touch a match to the oil. The messenger still defied him, and Bass commenced to count. When he had reached forty, Curley told him he would surrender, and accordingly opened the car door. He did this because the robbers were so situated that he and the guard could not fire upon them, and to remain in the car and let the robbers fire it would not save the property of the company at all, but, on the contrary, would cause the loss of much more property and be a needless sacrifice of his own life and that of the guard.

When the messenger surrendered and the car was opened, Bass entered and with cool audacity rifled it of what he could find, which, fortunately, was but little, as the messenger had secreted some valuable packages. The gang then went through the mail car, taking a few registered letters. When they entered the mail car, one of them remarked, "Uncle Billy" (meaning Mr. Wm. C. Towers, the route agent) "is getting old, but he must hurry up." How any of the gang knew the route agent is a mystery. The "butcher" boy on the train also participated in the fight, acting very gallantly, and when he came out on the platform of the car with pistol in hand, some one of the robbers remarked to him to "go back, we don't want any peanuts." For these reasons it has been contended that some of the party lived in Dallas, else how could they have known the name of the route agent and known who the "butcher" boy was. The probabilities are that it was Sam Pipes or Albert Herndon who made these remarks, for living near Mesquite and frequently at that place at train time, it would not be difficult for them to find out the name of the route agent, and persons of the "butcher" boys. It is believed that the "butcher" shot both Frank Jackson and Sam Pipes that night, for both were wounded with light bullets that did not more than break the skin, and the "butcher" had one of those little pet pistols calculated to irritate a man if he was shot with it and should find it out.

The firing aroused the few citizens of the place and some of them got up and armed themselves, not knowing, however, what was the matter, while others supposed it was only some of the wild boys of the country, the Scyene gang, perhaps, on a lark and firing off their pistols. Mr. Gross, a merchant of the place, proceeded towards the depot, with shot-gun in hand, and finding the fireman hid under the platform took him to be one of the robbers and made him hold up his hands. He then went as near the depot as he thought prudent, and then heard the robbers laughing and talking and having a pleasant time of it.

The robbers did not escape unscathed in that fight. Seaborn Barnes received four wounds, three in the right leg and one in the left thigh, all flesh wounds, but quite severe. Jackson was struck on the right shoulder with a ball from the "butcher's" little tomtit revolver, which barely broke the skin and fell down his sleeve, being caught by him in his hand and preserved as a curiosity and souvenir. Had it been from a six-shooter Mr. Jackson would have been placed *hors du combat* and captured and with the chances of recovery against him, for a shoulder shattered with gunshot is no light matter. Pipes was also wounded in the left side of the stomach, with the "butcher's" little pepper box, the wound being very slight. He would have been mortally wounded, sure, if the pistol he was shot with had been of any account. When it was reported to Bass that Sam Pipes was wounded, he responded, "Well, I can't help it; such things will happen. We've stayed here now, entirely too long." It was also reported that one of the "volunteers," who lived in the country near by, had been wounded in the fight, dying a day or two afterwards, but such was not the case. The rumor grew out of the fact that a young man whose parents resided in that neighborhood, a young man named Jenkins, was buried a day or two after the robbery, he having died of a gunshot wound. The facts in this young man's case were that he shot himself accidently at the residence of his brother-in-law, in Coleman County, while fooling with a pistol, and dying almost instantly. The certificate of the justice of the peace and the jury who held an inquest on the body and the affidavits of a large number of citizens of Coleman County attested the manner of his death, and because he was brought to his mother's home to be buried it was reported that he met his death at Mesquite. Barnes was so badly hurt that he could not ride far, but they managed to get him to Billie Collins' house, a few miles away, where he remained until his wounds were sufficiently healed for him to go back to the robber fastness in Denton County. His sumptuous apartment while at Billie Collins' was a hay-stack, which afforded him a comfortable bed, and secretion from the prying eyes of any person who might be nosing around.

It has been asked by a great many people why the convict guards did not go to the assistance of the train. Simply because the force was not strong enough to guard their prisoners and fight the robbers too, and the robbers had notified them that if they interfered at all they would turn the convicts loose. The amount of money obtained by the robbery was only about $160, a small sum for the risk taken and the damage sustained. Healy, the Windsor Hotel clerk, not only lost his hat, with a bullet hole in it, but was left behind by the train as well. One of the guards over the convicts started to the depot while the firing was going on, but was halted on the way, and fired at by a robber picket, and returning the fire, he returned to his post at the convict train. Bass and his "regulars," except Barnes, who remained at Billie Collins' house, as before stated, returned forthwith to their old haunts in Denton County, and the "volunteers" dispersed to their several homes in the neighborhood.

CHAPTER X

The Band

Short sketches of the members—a description of their
fastness in Denton County—An account of
some of their friends

THE ROBBERY of the train at Mesquite capped the climax. It seemed to be that every man in the county suddenly determined that the nefarious business should be stopped. The good name of Dallas County was beginning to suffer. Three out of four of the robberies had been committed in the confines of Dallas County, and the other one just over the line, in Collin County. The sheriff of Dallas County had no warrant or capias for the arrest of any person charged with train robbery, in fact no officer in the state had any legal papers for the arrest of anyone. It had just come to be known positively who the guilty parties were, and papers for their apprehension were being prepared and plans matured for their apprehension. The newspapers of the country were filled with sensational stories about the robbers and the denunciation of the authorities for not catching them. The Governor was roundly abused for not sending the entire force of state troops to the section where these depredations were committed, the most populous section of the state, too, and when it was urged that the civil authorities, with a *posse comitatus* of the state, were sufficient for the work and that the law did not contemplate the use of military force to execute the laws unless the civil authorities were powerless to do so. One paper in Dallas, cited by a man of exceeding valor in the retiracy of his sanctum, and noted chiefly for the bluster of his mental lucubrations, said, "To an awful hell with law and let State troops be sent here." Without the slightest conception of what the law was, without the remotest idea of what the power and authority of the *posse comitatus* (the presumption is, that he thought it was a writ), or of the effect of subrogating the civil to the military, he bellowed in his newspaper, like a bull of Bashan, for state troops to capture five highway robbers, and that, too, before the civil authorities had been able to take any steps towards their apprehension. But more upon the subject hereafter.

By this time it had become pretty generally known that Sam Bass and his party were the train robbers, and Sam and his thieves were on the alert, ready for a fight or a race and firm in the belief that they were invincible in their stronghold in the Cross Timbers in Denton County. It will not be amiss here to give short sketches of these bold bandits. We have already given the reader a short account of the life and history of Sam Bass from his birth up to his arrival in Denton County after the Big Springs robbery on the Union Pacific Railroad, and all who have read these pages up to this point have a pretty good idea of his doings and career after his arrival in Denton County up to this point in our narrative.

Second in command to Bass was Henry Underwood, and he was the brains of the party. He never lost his head, always weighed well every question, and calculated closely the chances of success in all undertakings of the band. He was Bass's mentor, and whenever his counsels were unheeded trouble ensued.

63

He was born in Jennings County, Indiana, on January 10th, 1846. His father and mother at last accounts were still living at the old homestead in Jennings County, Indiana, good people, well-to-do in the world and enjoying the respect and esteem of their entire community. Henry was well raised and given fair educational advantages and was, until he came to Texas, a useful, good citizen. When but a mere youth he was seized with the war fever, and joining a regiment from his section of Indiana, he entered the federal service at the very outbreak of hostilities. The wild and unrestrained life of a soldier was not at all beneficial to him, but developed all the worst elements of his character to such a degree that when troubles and temptations beset him in Denton County, he had not the firmness to resist and continue in the paths of virtue and rectitude. After the war was over, he settled in Kansas, and there married a most estimable young lady, who has clung to him throughout all his trials and difficulties with a devotion that ennobles her.

It has been said that Underwood killed a man in Kansas which led to his emigration to Texas, but this his wife strongly denies, declaring, and in this she is borne out by the evidence of people who knew him in Kansas, that he never had a difficulty of any kind before he came to Texas, but on the contrary was a sober, industrious, honest man, a good citizen who strove hard to build himself up in the world and who made his home happy by his love for it and affection for his wife. His wife was Miss Mary Emory, of Labeck County, Kansas, to whom he was united in marriage on the 10th day of January, 1871, his twenty-fifth birthday. He farmed while in Kansas and did well, because he was active and energetic and strictly attended to his business.

The Band

He removed from Kansas to Texas in September, 1871, located in the town of Denton. His first occupation was that of hauling wood to town, a business in which Gen. Grant was his great prototype. When he was not hauling wood, he was teaming between Denton and Dallas, and thereby earning an honest livelihood. About a year after his arrival at Denton, the lessons he learned during the war began to exert their influence. He was living in a little country town and in it were not a few young bloods addicted to card-playing, whisky-drinking, horse-racing, and ten-pin-rolling, and the association with these fell spirits seduced him from the steadiness of his ways. He began to grow dissolute in his habits, neglectful of business, and lacking in his duty to his young family. This occasioned his wife much trouble and distress, and, as he loved her ardently and yielded much to her influence, he would stop for spells his dissipated ways and buckle down to hard work, but he could not hold out. The trouble was that he lived in town. Had he made his home in the country and worked upon a farm, where he would have been aloof from the temptations that daily beset him, he would, today, have been a respected and honorable citizen of Texas.

In 1874 he and Sam Bass became warm friends and inseparable companions. Bass had just then gotten possession of his little race mare and started on the down grade that led to his final ruin, and Henry Underwood went along with him, stride for stride. After he started on his downhill course, he mostly frequented saloons, indulged in all kinds of dissipation and gambling whenever opportunity offered, and he soon became noted for recklessness. He manifested a remarkable antipathy for Negroes—we say remarkable because having been reared in Indiana, having fought to free the Negroes, and having lived in Kansas, where any sort of a Negro is better than a white man, the natural inference is that he would have had a warm feeling for the man and brother. He, however, had no love for the Negro, and seemed to act as though he felt that he had assisted in robbing the South of their Negroes and it was a duty he owed to keep them straight round about where he lived.

Negroes, as everyone knows, who has any knowledge of them, practical knowledge, not the sentimental lack-a-daisical estimate of the whining carpet-bagger or the pharisaical Republican of the North, will not pay their debts when they can help it. As God never made a Negro man or woman that will not steal nor a woman that will not sell her virtue for fifty cents or give it away if she can't get the money, it is their nature to defraud their creditors when they can. To stop their evil around Denton, Underwood made himself a sort of apostle. Whenever a darkey owed a little bill that was overdue, it was placed in Henry Underwood's hands for collection, and he always got the money. He did not care whether the Negro had the money or not, he had to pay the bill or take the consequences, and those consequences were not of the pleasantest nature.

His *modus operandi* when he had one of these bills to collect was to go to the Negro's house about midnight, and calling him out he would say to him: "You are owing Mr. —— some money. He has given me the bill for collection and I want you to pay it. I will be here at midnight tomorrow night, and if you have not got the money off comes the top of your head," and he would press the muzzle of a six-shooter to the Negro's forehead to impress him with the importance of his words.

Promptly at midnight he would call on the Negro again, and just as promptly he would receive the money that was due.

He was five feet nine inches high, dark complected, black hair, small keen black or dark brown eyes, set deep in their sockets. He always wore a mustache rather dark in color and heavy. He always stood straight and erect, was of nervous temperament, a frolicsome disposition, and very quick to anger and reckless in resenting affronts. When excited his voice was loud and shrill, and while he had a courage that knew no fear, yet he was cunning as a fox, prudent and shrewd. He was always ready for anything venturesome and stopped not for scruples, still he was kind at heart and not at all blood-thirsty. There is no doubt that it is to him that many a good citizen of Denton County owes his life, for when Bass and his other confederates were exasperated and being pursued from pillar to post, they wanted to wreck vengeance on those citizens they believed to be assisting the officers, but Underwood always counseled to the contrary and restrained them from adding murder to their other crimes.

On one occasion, not long after he and Bass had become so intimate, they had a difficulty in the town of Denton with some Negroes. They had been herding some cattle for a few days prior to that, and being in town, Bass bought a watermelon, which he was carrying before him on his horse to camp, but the horse becoming unruly, he dropped it, bursting it open. These Negroes were lounging about near by and they set up a boisterous laugh at the accident. This irritated them so that they both dismounted and let fly a shower of stones at the darkies. One Negro, Albert Wilson, was severely hurt by a blow on the head and all the Negroes ran off save one, a preacher named

Sterling Johnson, who stood his ground. Underwood tackled him with a club and was about to brain him, but seeing who it was resisted with the remark, "I've a good notion to knock your damned head off, Sterling. If you were not a good Negro, I'd kill you, damn you." He and Bass then proceeded out of town on a full gallop, but returning shortly afterwards, Deputy Sheriff Tom Gerren attempted to arrest Underwood, but he retreated and Gerren fired at him as he ran. He and Bass proceeded to camp, where they with two other cowboys who sided with them defied arrest. A posse was sent after them, but could not find them, as they fell back into Hickory Creek bottom. This was the first open defiance of the law by these men, and he and Bass soon left the country.

When Underwood left Denton, he went out toward Ft. Concho and while at Concho he got into a difficulty with an organization of cattle vigilantes who had undertaken to regulate the cattle business in that section, or in other words, look after thieves. He did not like the organization and was very free spoken in characterizing it as a mob, and one day while expressing himself in a saloon concerning some of the members of the organization, some of them attempted to make him hush. He was not that kind of metal, and a fearful melee ensued. He shot two of the vigilantes and was himself desperately wounded with a Winchester rifle ball which passed through his body. The people were greatly exasperated. Wounded as he was, he eluded pursuit for a time by hiding in the brush, but was finally captured. Had he not been so dangerously wounded, he would have graced a post oak limb, but his captors, believing that he was mortally wounded and could live but a short time, refrained from lynching him and carried him to the hospital at the fort to die quietly.

One of the men he had shot was also in the hospital with his arm badly broken near the shoulder and they had some very animated discussions as they lay on their couches, both helpless. Henry had no thought of dying himself, but he encouraged his captors to believe that he would, and daily grew feebler and apparently nearer his end, and just as his captors were thinking that he could last but a little while longer and were therefore careless in their watchfulness of him, he disappeared from the hospital. Procuring a horse, he sped for Denton County where he could have the loving attention and tender care of his wife, for he was really badly wounded and still in a dangerous condition.

This experience seemed somewhat to have taught him a lesson, for when he recovered from his wound, he went to work and was living a sober, industrious life until he was arrested on suspicion of burning the Presbyterian Church in which court was held in the town of Denton. Of this charge there is no doubt now but he was entirely innocent. But he had led such a wild life and was known to be so reckless and so devoted to his friends that the theory was advanced that he had fired the building to destroy the indictments and records in the court against some of his friends, and upon this theory he was taken into custody and imprisoned, as he was unable to give bond. He was kept in close confinement in jail for six months in Denton and Gainesville, and then discharged and the indictment that had been found against him dismissed for lack of evidence.

This wrong accusation and imprisonment embittered him and aroused the Ishmael in his nature and made him more reckless than ever. It was but a short time until he got into a difficulty about a yoke of oxen and an affidavit was made against him for the theft of the oxen. He, however, had experience enough in the Denton County jail and avoided arrest in this instance. This was another wrongful charge. He may have been in the wrong from a strict point in the oxen case, but he had color of title to them and believed they equitably belonged to him, and when he took possession of them it was not a case of theft; it had none of the elements of a felony about it, and the charge of theft was but another act to harden him on to desperation. We have no apologies to make for the crimes committed by Underwood, and having nothing to advance to screen him from that justice at the hands of the law that he so richly deserves, but even a dog is entitled to a fair statement of all the circumstances connected with his career, be it ever so evil. The wrongs that were done him were brought upon himself by himself indirectly, and even if they had not been, if he had never done anything to forfeit the respect and esteem of his fellow-men, and had not been the unfortunate victim of fortuitous circumstances, his misfortunes were not a justification for his career of crime and wickedness, and that fate which the stern decrees of law may yet mete out to him will be just, and Henry Underwood in his own strong good sense knows it.

When he left his home and his family to evade arrest for the charge of stealing the oxen, he at once joined his fortunes with those of Sam Bass, who was in camp at Cove Hollow, in Denton County, near the Cooke County line, having but a little while before returned from the scene of the Big Springs robbery on the Union Pacific Railroad. This was about the middle of November, '77, and as Bass had an abundance of gold, he purchased two horses from Jim Murphy, and he and Underwood and Frank Jackson,

70

who had also just joined him, went to San Antonio.

Sheriff Everheart, of Grayson County, and Sheriff Eagan, of Denton County, had just received the news of Bass's complicity in the Union Pacific Railroad robbery, and the former and Tom Gerren, one of Sheriff Eagan's deputies, followed them to San Antonio, in company with one Tony Waits, a detective, both Bass and Underwood being the game Everheart and Waits were after, they believing that Underwood was the Tom Nixon of the Big Springs robbery crowd, but Gerren was only after Bass, being ignorant of the fact that Everheart and Waits wanted Underwood also until they arrived at San Antonio. Everheart knew of Underwood's wild and reckless course in Denton County and of the intimacy existing between him and Bass, and as he answered pretty well the description furnished him of Tom Nixon, he believed Underwood to be the man. When Gerren was informed of these suspicions and the intentions of Everheart and Waits, he hooted at the idea, because he said that he knew of his own knowledge that Underwood was not connected with the Union Pacific robbery, for he was in Denton County and stayed all night at the house of a friend of Gerren in September, a night or two before the Big Springs robbery. Everheart and Gerren fell out over this matter and no arrest was made in San Antonio. Bass stated that he and his friends were on a big hurrah in San Antonio and that they never knew the officers were after them, although Jackson met Gerren one day and shook hands with him. After their spree was over, they returned to Denton County, having been absent some weeks, and Bass took up at his old headquarters in Cove Hollow.

Underwood went to visit his family, and on the night of December 24th, 1877, Everheart and posse surrounded his house, and closing in on it early the next morning, demanded Underwood to surrender, as he was authorized to arrest him as Tom Nixon. Underwood protested that he was not Nixon, and said he did not propose to surrender. Being assured that there was a man in the party' who would swear that he was the Tom Nixon of the Big Springs robbery, and seeing that resistance was vain, he surrendered and was conveyed to Kearney, Nebraska, and there lodged in jail. This was the third charge that had been wrongfully made against Underwood, and the second time that he had been unjustly arrested, and it cut deeply into his soul. There never was the slightest grounds for suspecting Underwood of being Nixon, and the detective who misled Sheriff Everheart, and who was so ready to swear to Underwood's identity as Nixon, no doubt had a keen eye on the $500 reward which it has been said was paid by the Express Company.

As before stated, Underwood escaped from the Kearney jail, and reaching Denton, he at once linked his fortunes with those of Bass. The Mesquite robbery being the first and only one of the train robberies in which he participated, though he was accessory to the Eagle Ford robbery. His history from this point is identified with the operations of the Bass desperadoes.

The next member of the gang in point of importance was Frank Jackson. He was born on the 10th of June, 1856, some of his friends say in Wise County, but his relatives say in Llano County, Texas. His father and mother were both pious members of the Methodist church and most exemplary people. His father was a hardworking blacksmith, and by the sweat of his brow at daily toil, earned an honest livelihood for his family. His father, Robert Jackson, died in 1863, when Frank was but seven

years old, and his mother, Phoebe, died in 1864, a little
less than a year afterwards, leaving him at this tender age
without parental care, guidance, and counsel. He had
two sisters and two brothers, who, with himself, were taken
in charge by Joseph Barker, his mother's brother. Mr.
Barker was in limited circumstances, and as the children
inherited little or no property from their father's and
mother's estates, he was unable to give them but little
educational advantages, and living in the frontier portion
of the state, there were but few advantages to offer, had
he been able to give them. The consequence was that
young Jackson grew up uncultured and unrestrained, with
no examples about him to pattern after, save the wild
and uncouth cowboys, and rough frontiersmen with whom
he came in contact. The society was not such as to expand
the character of a youth, himself high spirited and full of
animal courage and vim which makes strong good men
when properly directed into one of gentleness and tracta-
bility. Raised without restraint, he grew up to have an
abhorrence of it, and an utter contempt for the trammels
of society and of law. Yet with all this he was a young
man of kind disposition, of a liberal nature and full of
energy. He had all the elements within him to have made
an excellent citizen, a worthy man, and leading spirit for
good, had he been trained in his youth as he should have
been, and surrounded with influences to mould aright his
character. From Llano County, the uncle and guardian
moved to Arkansas, remaining a short time, and in 1871
they came back to Texas, settling in Denton County, the
children finding homes in different families. Frank, then
fifteen years of age, found employment with Dr. R. S.
Ross, a most estimable gentleman, who took an interest
in the youth because of his sprightliness, his industry and

fidelity to every trust imposed in him. He remained with Dr. Ross some time, when he went to live with Mr. Ben A. Key, who had married one of his sisters, and with him learned the tinner's trade.

Mr. Key, a worthy, good citizen, influenced Frank to study at night, and he soon gained a fair knowledge of the rudiments of English, learning to read and spell fairly, and to write a plain hand. But his nature was restless, and confinement of work at the tinner's bench was irksome to him, he longed for the freedom of the cattle trail, and the open air of country life. It was not because he was averse to work, for he could not be idle, preferring to do any kind of labor to doing nothing, nor was he inclined to dissipation, or frolicking, but there was a seething cauldron of unrest in his bosom all the time, generated by the free life he had led in his childhood and youth on horseback, herding cattle or working on a farm. It soon became so irksome to him to labor at his bench, cooped up in a house all day, that he broke through the thralls that restrained him and found vent for the effervescence of spirits within him by frequenting billiard halls and drinking saloons of Denton, and then it was but a step to drinking, and gambling soon followed as a matter of course.

Unfortunately for Frank, there was a desperate, lawless Negro, named Henry Goodall, living in Denton County. This Negro was always committing some petty depredations, never went unarmed, was quarrelsome and overbearing, and continually involved in a broil with the people of his own color, or with some white man. He was a fearless character, and would as soon have a difficulty with a white man as a black one, and made himself a terror to the whole community. In the fall of 1876, Goodall obtained possession of a horse claimed by Jackson, and a row ensued between them over the horse. Frank told him he had to return the horse, or replace it with another, else he would kill him. Finally the Negro promised to give him another horse for the one in question, and the two went out on the prairie to get the animal. When night came, neither of the men returned home, but the Negro's horse returning with blood on the saddle and bridle, search was instituted for Goodall by the Negroes, and the next day about nine o'clock in the morning his body was found on the prairie with a pistol bullet in his brain, and his throat cut from ear to ear.

Jackson, at this time, having quit the tinning business, was herding cattle for Jim Murphy, who had a ranche in the northeastern edge of Denton County. When he was found during the day of the discovery of Goodall's body, he was at Murphy's herding camp, and unhesitatingly said he had killed the Negro. His version of the affair was that while he and Goodall were looking for the horses, they came across a hole of water, and he got off his horse to get a drink, and while he was stooping to drink, the Negro drew his pistol remarking, "I've got you now where I wanted you," and immediately fired at him, but missed him. That he, Jackson, then jumped up and drawing his pistol, returned the fire, wounding the Negro in the side. He mounted his horse at once and a running fight ensued, in which he shot the Negro in the forehead, killing him. The throat cutting he never had anything to say about. The Negro was shot in the side, and his six-shooter empty.

There was no evidence against Jackson, except his own statement, and as that was insufficient to convict him of killing Goodall, a man of desperate character as he bore in the country, he was never indicted. It would have been better for Jackson for him to have been arrested and tried for this offence, and would have been a vindication of the law as well. A trial and thorough investigation of the case would have inspired him with respect for the law, and would have impressed him with the enormity of taking human blood. As it was, it only made him more reckless, more indifferent to the restraints of the law, and he was emboldened to embark into fresh schemes of lawlessness.

He remained in the service of Murphy as a cowboy for near a year after the bloody episode in his life, and then returned to the town of Denton, and to work again at his trade of tinner, with his brother-in-law, Ben A. Key. In November, 1877, Sam Bass returned to Denton County, from the scene of his exploits of robbing the express train at Big Springs, on the Union Pacific Railroad, and had been in the county but a short time before he began to make overtures to Frank Jackson to join him. He knew Jackson well, had caroused with him in the saloons of Denton, knew his bold, reckless, fearless spirit, and he wanted him because he knew he could rely upon him in any trying hour. Bass began his persuasions upon Jackson, was liberal with his stolen gold, spending it freely for liquor, and keeping Frank constantly supplied with money. He painted in glowing colors the pleasures of the life of a bandit, and the ease with which they made money, and finally when he offered Jackson $100 per month in gold to go with him, he resisted the entreaties of his sister and other relatives, and putting aside all compunctions, joined the outlaw. He was at this time a little past twenty-one years of age, was six feet high, his complexion was sunburned, his hair a light brown and a dark blue eye in his head that flashed intelligence and the subdued light of an invincible spirit. He was smooth-faced and looked more

76

like a stripling of eighteen than a man just entering upon the threshold of his majority. He was of a negative-positive nature. He could be led and persuaded into anything, but no moral force could drive him. He was utterly deficient in moral purpose and could be tempted into any deed of deviltry or daring. He was in every one of the train robberies committed in Texas, except the one at Eagle Ford, but at that time he was suffering of a stricken conscience and was wavering between Bass and his duty to society, to his family and himself. His relatives were pleading with him to abandon the life he had entered upon, and he had well nigh determined to do so, but unfortunately, had a collision with a party of express detectives from Dallas, near Denton, of which more will be said further on in this book. This encounter, in which shots were exchanged, hardened him in his career, for he then realized that an outraged law was about to redress its wrongs, and that he was under a ban. He saw no hope for himself but to cling to his "pals" and fight it out with them against the law. He had gone too far to retreat, and there was no fate left to him but to go on, and on to the ending, where he would be finally swallowed up in the maelstrom of a relentless fate his own hand had wrought. He never wavered from his fealty to Bass from this day on, and in every peril was by his side, and was the last of all the old gang to part with him, and only then it was when the dews of death were dampening his leader's brow, and officers of the law hot at their heels.

Seaborn Barnes was next on the roll of bandits, not because of reliability, or extraordinary efficiency, because Seaborn wore a white feather in his hat, but in point of enlistment. He was born in Tarrant County, of respectable parentage, about 1853. He turned cowboy when a mere youth, and grew up with the wild, rough men, who lived about isolated cattle ranches, and follow the cattle trail. The "cowboy" is a character unto himself, and peculiar to Texas. He grows up in the wilds like the Texas half-breed horses, and Texas cattle, without restraint of any kind, without knowledge of the uses and demands of society, and knows nothing of the law except what little he may hear of it at long range, or learn of it when he comes within its grasp for some violation of its behests. He is a law unto himself and despises the fundamental rule and spirit that fills statute books. He not only despises it, but regards it as a tyranny and outrageous invasion of the rights of man. As a class, cowboys are generous to a fault, true as steel in their friendships, and bitter even unto death to their enemies. Full of courage, almost remarkably, he is ready to do and dare at all times, and scorns danger in all its forms. Broad-brimmed hats, fancy-topped boots, bright-colored shirts, big spurs, fiery, high-headed horses are their pride and joy. Living on horseback almost all the time, sleeping out in all kinds of weather, they are hardy and rugged of constitution, and stand any manner of privation and hardship. When they come into the settlements, they feel out of place as it were, feel constrained, and filling up with raw whisky, their chief delight is to show their contempt for the trammels of society, and to raise a "rookus." They are not vehemently bad, but are simply illustrations of energy, vim, and courage, and animal spirits unconfined and gone to riot.

With this class of men young Barnes grew up and in their companionship his character was moulded. About the first and only fixed business he ever had, other than cowboy, was when he worked at the potter's trade with Mr. A. H. Serrens, about five miles from the town of

Denton, a short time. He was tall and slender in build, with a high, broad forehead, a roman nose, dark, hazel eyes, his brow overhanging them like a beetling cliff, and from his cheek-bones down to his chin, his face narrowed rapidly, giving it a peaked look. His neck was remarkably long and scraggy, and he had an unusually large Adam's apple in his throat. He was rough and uncouth in manner, and very illiterate. There were few redeeming traits in the character of Barnes, for he was wanting in courage, and was brutal in his instincts, and of repulsive address.

Barnes was in all the train robberies, unless it was Eagle Ford, in which one it is probable he did not participate, according to the account of Sam Bass. At Mesquite, he received the bullet wounds, an account of which we have already given. He remained with his captain up to the day of his death, he being the first to fall in the fight at Round Rock, on the 10th of July, 1878, being shot through the head with a Winchester rifle ball, by R. C. Ware, one of the Texas Rangers.

The last on the list of regulars was "Arkansaw" Johnson, and Bass had no better man in his ranks for a deed of infamy or of daring than this same "Arkansaw" Johnson. Not a great deal is known of the life of this man prior to his joining Sam Bass. Henry Underwood formed his acquaintance in the jail at Kearney, Nebraska, and it was through Johnson's wife, or mistress, that they were enabled to escape from the Kearney jail. Underwood induced him to come to Texas with him, and it is generally believed that he never had operated in this state before. He had done good work at the service of the devil in Arkansas, and it was for this reason that he was given the soubriquet of "Arkansaw" by his companion thieves on the western plains. He was an Irishman by birth, was about thirty-five years of age at the time of his death; was five feet eight inches high, of heavy build, florid complexion, had cold steel-blue eyes, light hair, and rather heavy sun-burnt beard of a brownish tinge. He was dish faced, pox marked, and extremely repulsive in appearance, brutish in his instincts, cruel, vindictive, overbearing, remorseless, and utterly indifferent to danger. He was as utterly devoid of conscientious compunctions, or scruples, as the most hardened villain that "ever cut a throat or scuttled a ship."

His real name was Huckston, and he served during the war in a federal regiment, and whenever opportunity offered was skulking through the country foraging on the people, hesitating not even at murder for the sake of booty. He was mustered out of the federal service in Arkansas after the close of the war, and the lessons of iniquity he had acquired while in the army he retained. He had some money when he was mustered out, which he squandered soon in riotous living, and then he began a course of petty stealing to replenish his pocket book, but after a little while this did not satisfy his recklessness, daring spirit, and he began a course of highway robbery and horse stealing, associating with him a few as daring scoundrels as himself, and it was not long until he became a terror to two or three counties along the Arkansas River.

Finally, he stayed all night with an old man named Wilberforce, whose family consisted only of himself, his aged wife, and a daughter, a beautiful young girl just blooming into womanhood. She was as lovely a girl as there was in all Arkansas, accomplished, cultured, and refined, and she was the belle of all the neighborhood. Her father had a handsome home, filled with all the comforts of life, as well as many of its luxuries, and it was his pleasure to gratify the aesthetic tastes of his daughter. Consequently his yards and conservatory were marvelous in the richness of their rare flowers and plants; the walls of his parlor, his library, and his dining room were adorned with choice and tasteful selections of art; sculptuary filled niches in his halls and gleamed amid grottoes on his premises; and his daughter, being a skilled musician, music ravished the air with its melody from time to time to fill up the measure of home's happiness. It was an abiding place to fill with delight the soul of the voluptuary. It was reputed that the old man Wilberforce had a considerable amount of money about the house, and it was known that the daughter possessed magnificent and costly jewelry of precious stones. Johnson determined to rob the old man, and for that purpose arrived at his house about dark and craved his hospitality, and with that nature so peculiar to the southern gentleman, he welcomed the miscreant to the shelter of his home and the bounties of his table. Johnson was well dressed, and assuming as best he could the role of a gentleman, he was treated as one. After a sumptuous supper, he was invited into the parlor, where the daughter played upon the piano for him, and sang for him, and entertained him in so charming a manner that his bosom became influenced with a fierce and unholy passion, which he determined to gratify before the rising of the morning's sun. Soon feigning fatigue, he was shown to his room, a more elegant and luxurious apartment than he ever before had entered, and retired at once, not to slumber, but to think over a plan for carrying into effect his hellish intentions.

In the country, people always retire early, and in warm weather they generally leave their doors and windows open, and this was the case at the Wilberforce house. By nine o'clock the whole family were slumbering sweetly, dreaming of no danger, and two of them never to wake again in this world. About ten o'clock, Johnson arose stealthily, and leaving his room, soon found the whereabouts of the family. The old man and his wife were asleep in a room a few doors from his, the door opening on the hallway wide open, and in a room next to them, the daughter was sleeping, her room door ajar and the blinds to the window closed. The murderer settled at once upon his plan of action. Procuring a heavy iron, he crept on tiptoe to the old man's bedside, and with one fearful blow, he crushed in his skull, the old man dying immediately with only a stifled moan. The dull thud of the blow, and the dying moan of her husband slightly disturbed the old lady and she stirred, but if awakened, before she could give outcry, Johnson had given her a blow with his cruel iron bar that sent her soul to eternity on the instant.

He then proceeded cautiously to the daughter's room. The night was warm, and she having her window blinds closed, she had lain down on her bed with only an undergarment on, with swelling bosom and beautiful limbs, all unveiled and the shining summer zephyrs kissed and dallied with very wantoness. A waning moon shed a dim radiance through the room, and Johnson, all thoughtless of the silent deed in the room adjoining, utterly indifferent to the terrible deed he had just committed, gazed in brutish ecstacy upon the beauteous form that lay in innocence before him, and gloated with the savage passions of an animal upon the charms he saw. The blood leaped like molten fire through his veins and his breath came and went in short deep sighs, and in his eagerness he could scarcely constrain himself. With trembling hands, he drew from his pocket a bottle of chloroform, with which he was always provided, and saturating a sponge, held it gently to her nose so she would only get partially under the influence of the insidious drug. He only wanted her to become partially insensible, just enough for him to bind her securely by her feet and wrist, and gag her to prevent her outcry when her terrible awakening should come. Having done this, he proceeded to outrage the helpless girl, he having in the meantime procured a light. During this fearful ordeal, the young girl regained her consciousness; and no imagination can conceive, no heart realize, her horror. The beautiful black eyes that had been wont to flash with intelligence, to melt with the soft and tender look of love, were now dilated with terror, and almost bursting from their sockets in affright. In vain did she attempt to scream, for the sound was muffled in her throat only to die unheard, in vain did she writhe her body and limbs, and strain on the cruel gyves that bound her, for they would not yield. Again and again did the infamous wretch force his filthy embraces upon her until reason left its throne, and she lay upon her couch, she who had lain down to slumber innocent in thought, pure in heart, happy in the love of parents, whose idol she was; she, the belle of society, the favored favorite of the community, lay upon her couch, orphaned, a maniac, her body defiled and all bleeding and torn, her life ruined, never again to know joy or happiness. Oh! it was a pitiable sight, a sight to make a heart of stone to bleed. Better had Johnson slain her too. Less cruel it would have been to have crushed her skull with his iron bar as he had done the father and mother, than to leave her as he did, a mad creature, horror haunted ever after, with the shadow of an awful terror upon her soul, and the agony of a ceaseless fear in her heart.

Having satiated his beastly desires, he proceeded to rifle trunks and bureaus, but found only a few hundred dollars in money, and the diamonds of the young lady, worth some $3,000, which he wrenched from their settings, and then going and taking a last look at the wretched girl, he left her bound as she was, extinguished the lights in the room, and procuring a luncheon from the pantry, got his horse and left. He knew that it would not do for him to remain in Arkansas after this, for his judgment told him the crimes might be traced to him. He proceeded rapidly to Missouri, and thence over into Kansas, whence he drifted out on the plains.

The Negroes from the quarter, the house servants, found the dead bodies of the old man and woman, and the young lady still bound and gagged, the next morning early, and giving the alarm, the neighborhood was soon aroused, and a party on the trail of Johnson, but not being able to follow it, he escaped. The most intense excitement ensued, and strenuous efforts were made for months, and large rewards offered to effect the discovery and arrest of the perpetrator of the fearful crimes, but in vain. The young lady was a raving maniac, and was sent to the state lunatic asylum, where she lingered a few years until death happily removed her to a better and brighter lot.

Johnson, when in his cups on one occasion, told a companion of this crime, and it has since his death become public. He was in the Eagle Ford and Mesquite robberies, and although he was rather despised by Bass, Jackson, and Barnes at first, it was with reluctance that he was admitted, only Henry Underwood's influence prevailing that he be taken in on probation, as it were, he proved himself equal to any emergency by his *sang froid* in danger, and his reckless daring. Bass regretted that he did not take his advice on two occasions. Johnson was a fine judge of human nature, and the first time Will Scott ever came into their camp, he declared that he was a spy, and urged Bass to put him out of the way, which was unheeded by the robber chief, and afterwards deeply deplored. Johnson also urged immediately after the Mesquite robbery that the gang slip quietly out of the country and go to Arkansas, and rob a bank. He argued that it would be better to do this than to stay and brave the law and its officers, as it would only be a question of time before they would be killed, captured, or driven off. But Bass would not listen to this advice either, and greatly regretted it afterwards when beset with trials and troubles incident to the campaigne made against him by the officers of the law.

Johnson remained with his chosen leader, ably and courageously seconding him in all his difficulties, until death overtook him on the 12th of June, 1878, in the Salt Creek fight in Wise County, with Captain June Peak and his Rangers, he being shot by Sergeant Thomas A. Floyd, of the Rangers, a citizen of Dallas County.

We have given brief sketches of the regulars here, and will have something to say of the volunteers, Billie Collins, Sam Pipes, and Albert Herndon, who assisted in the Mesquite robbery, and of Charlie Carter and Henry Collins, who joined them after the robberies, and of Jim Murphy the informer, Will Scott the detective, and Scott Mayes, suspected of being *particeps criminis* with the outlaws, Wm. Miner, a detective, and others, suspected and arrested as accessories and accomplices, as we proceed with the narrative.

This is rather a lengthy chapter, but we trust it has been an interesting one. It ought certainly to point a moral, and teach the lesson that crime always reaps a terrible retribution, that wherever the laws of God and man are violated and outraged, that sure disgrace, ignominy, sorrow, desolation, and destruction are sure to follow.

CHAPTER XI

Bass First Suspected

*The first steps taken to ferret out the robbers—A funny
fiasco near Denton—Hot on the trail, and lively
times in the Cross Timbers—Running
fights and death to horse flesh*

IT WILL be remembered that the robbery of the Union
Pacific train, at Big Springs Station, Nebraska, by Joel
Collins, Sam Bass, and Co., was on the 19th of September,
1877. Bass arrived safely in Denton County after this
robbery, the first of November following, and about the
middle of that month he and Underwood and Jackson
went to San Antonio. The express and railroad companies
knew the names and had a description of all the robbers
in the Big Springs affair, and had not only sent the same
to officers in Texas, but had also sent a detective, "so
called," one "Toony" Waits, into the state to shadow Sam
Bass and Nixon, as they believed the latter had come to
Texas with Sam.

Sheriff Everheart, of Grayson County, with whom the
immortal "Toony" was operating, ascertaining that Bass
and Underwood and Jackson had gone to San Antonio,
followed them, as has before been stated, with Tom Gerren,
deputy sheriff of Denton County, who was also posted as
to Bass, to effect the capture of Bass and Underwood,
believing Underwood to be the Tom Nixon of the Big

KILLING OF COLLINS AND HEFFRIDGE

Springs robbery, but Gerren knew that Underwood was not in that robbery, and a squabble ensuing, neither of the parties were arrested. We say this much by way of preface, to show that the sheriffs of Grayson and Denton counties and their deputies knew, for three months prior to the first train robbery in Texas, that Sam Bass was one of the Big Springs robbers, yet they neither arrested him nor suspected him, it seems, of the Texas train robberies at first. Not only did they know that Bass was one of the Big Springs robbers, but they knew also that, about the 20th of December, 1877, the stage coach running between Fort Worth and Cleburne was stopped and robbed by highwaymen, and that about the middle of February the stage coach between Fort Worth and Weatherford was robbed, and still knowing Bass to be a highwayman, and in the country, he was not suspected.

Just after the Hutchins train robbery, say the latter part of March, 1878, Sheriff Eagan, of Denton County, began to lay plans for the capture of Bass for his participation in the Union Pacific robbery, and to that end, engaged a man named Wm. Miner to go into Bass's camp in the Cross Timbers and ensnare him to some point where he could effect his arrest. It was understood between Eagan, his deputies, and United States Commissioner Alexander Robertson that Miner was engaged upon this work. To facilitate him in his endeavors to gain the confidence of Bass and to gain for himself free ingress to, and egress from, Bass's camp, Miner cultivated the acquaintance of a man named Scott Mayes, who ran a saloon in Denton, and was on intimate terms with Bass, and whose partner in the saloon business it was generally believed he was. Mayes visited Bass whenever he desired to do so and often received Bass at his saloon in the lone hours of

Sam Bass

the night. Mayes, after the hunt for Bass became general, claimed that he was also a spy on Bass and trying to effect his capture for the sake of the rewards, but this does not seem to have ever been fully authenticated. At any rate, Mayes was fully posted as to the true inwardness of all Bass's operations, and through him Miner learned a number of things of interest concerning the freebooters, which were duly reported to Sheriff Eagan.

The first definite plan agreed upon for the capture of Bass was as follows: Mayes informed Bass that a Polander named Paul Agus, keeping a little grocery store in Denton, had $2,300 in money, which he kept in a trunk in his bedroom upstairs over his store. Bass and his companions were to come into Denton on a certain night and at a certain hour were to go to the Polander's room and overpowering him, were to take the money. Mayes was to be in the room with the Polander that night on some pretended business, and when the robbers came he was to be greatly terrified and captured along with the victim, and after the crowd left was to make a great hue and cry and get the officers after them. Miner, who was on to the scheme, posted Sheriff Eagan, who intended to be all ready to bag his game. In the meantime, before this burglary and theft was to be carried into effect, Bass and "Arkansaw" Johnson, with two unknown assistants, had robbed the train at Eagle Ford, and the next day after the robbery, April the 5th, Jim Curry, a detective in the employ of the Texas and Pacific Railroad, and Sam Finley, in the employ of the Texas Express Company, and two other men with them, had struck a hot trail leading towards Denton County, and had followed it into that county, and when within about three miles of Denton came suddenly upon the men asleep near the roadside.

They had ridden by them, when someone in the party discovered their horses picketed near. The men beside the road discovered Curry and his party about the same time, and, seeing them halt, fired upon them, Curry returning the fire, no one being hurt on either side. Hostilities then ceased and a conversation ensued between the two parties. Curry and his men did not know that these were the men they were after and did not want to shoot them, and while they were talking with them, the men, who were Henry Underwood and Frank Jackson, saddled their horses and mounting them, dashed off with a whoop into the dense woods. Curry and his party were non-plussed at first, and supposing that these were but the picket guards of a considerable gang, they did not pursue them, but sought more force.

A correspondent from Denton to the *Dallas Herald* says of Curry and his party: "Continuing on to Denton, they stopped at the Lacy House on Saturday afternoon (once the home of Bass). While there, the notorious Sam Bass and a number of his associates appeared on the outskirts and, according to one statement, rode into the city. They had heard that the Dallas party were looking for outlaws, and were anxious to know if they were the men whom they sought; if so, they would like to have them come out and try to take them. Messengers galloped back and forth between the excited and defiant crowd and their friends in the city. Finally, later in the evening, Bass and company sent a messenger to the Dallas men to inform them that they would remain in sight of them two hours and a half, and challenged them to come out and fight. They stood near the residence of John A. Lovejoy, Jr., in the eastern suburbs of the city, plain to the view from the public square. More than a hundred saw them."

The most of this statement is purely imaginative, the creation of the correspondent's fancy. Some of the Bass gang, Underwood, Jackson, and Barnes, did ride into the suburbs of Denton, but they sent no messengers, defied nobody, but, on the contrary, as soon as they ascertained that their presence was known, they made a bee line for tall timber as rapidly as their horses could carry them, and Sheriff Eagan, and a posse armed with shot guns in hot pursuit, were unable to get in sight of them. Curry and his party did not join in the pursuit, for the reason that both themselves and their horses were worn out, and as they had work ahead of them, they preferred rest. They would not lend their arms either, because they could not tell when Sheriff Eagan and his party would return, and they would need them themselves when they had recuperated. It has been said that Captain June Peak was with this party of Curry's, but this is a mistake. He was in Dallas County organizing a force to carry into execution plans of his own for the capture of the train robbers. We have given minutely an account of the above transactions, because they defeated Sam Bass's plan to rob the Polander in Denton, and prevented Eagan from effecting capture then.

Up to this time but one man had suspected Bass and his gang of being the perpetrators of the Texas train robberies. From the day the news was received of the first robbery at Allen Station, on the 22nd of February, he settled upon Bass as the head of the gang. He knew that Bass was in the Union Pacific robbery, and, as never before had any railroad train been robbed in Texas, he naturally concluded that it was Bass who had inaugurated this species of outlawry, especially as the first robbery was within easy striking distance of Bass's stronghold, and as he had about him a gang of men who would follow him in his lawless undertaking.

At this time Captain Peak was recorder of the city of Dallas, and having been city marshal prior to that, in which position he made distinction for himself as a bold and efficient officer and as a detective of rare skill, the Texas Express Company induced him to resign his office as city recorder, and take service with them as a detective. This was just before the Hutchins robbery, and immediately after that affair, in pursuance of his theory that Bass and his gang were committing the outrages, he took with him James McGinley, a citizen of Dallas, and quietly went up into Denton County, more to gain information and ascertain if he was correct in his surmises than anything else.

When he reached the Cross Timbers, in which Bass had his stronghold and through which he and his fellows roamed at random and with impunity, as did Robin Hood and his merry men through Sherwood Forest, he found that it would be necessary for him to have a guide through its trackless wastes and dense fastnesses, so he hired a boy about sixteen years old named Tommy Stout. After he and McGinley had been in the timbers a few days, they stopped one afternoon to get a drink of water and to rest at the house of Green Hill, and while there, two men rode by whom Hill told them were Bass and Underwood, and that they were going to Bob Murphy's. Soon after they left Hill's, Captain Peak sent the boy on to Murphy's and told him to stay all night if Bass or none of the gang was there, but if they were, to come on to the crossing of the Elm Fork of the Trinity, where he and McGinley would await him, and if he stayed all night to meet them at sun-up the next morning at the crossing of the river. The boy stayed all night, and when Captain Peak met him the next morning he asked him what he saw and heard. The boy stated that when he got to Murphy's, Bass and all his men were there, and that Green Hill came, too, shortly afterwards. That the whole party stayed all night, persuading him to stay too. They wanted to know what he was doing with June Peak and McGinley, riding around through the timbers. They then told him they didn't want to hurt him, and for him to go home, for just as sure as he went riding through the woods with them that day he would be killed along with them. Captain Peak asked him what he was going to do, and he said he was going home, and home he went.

Captain Peak had gotten by that time all the information he thought he could get—enough to satisfy him that Bass and his party were the train robbers—and furthermore that the Murphys and Green Hill were friends of the Bass party, and if they were not accessories to the robberies, they harbored them and procured supplies for them. He and McGinley then returned to Dallas, shortly after which the Eagle Ford robbery occurred. Captain Peak was the first man to suspect Bass and the first one to direct efforts toward his capture for the Texas train robberies. Sheriff Eagan continued his efforts to capture Bass for the Union Pacific robbery, and in this interest, Miner and Scott Mayes a few days after the fiasco near Denton, before described, set out for the region of Hickory Creek to find Captain Bass and company. Being unsuccessful in their search, they stopped at Green Hill's house, where they were introduced to Billie Collins, and shortly afterwards starting on their return to Denton, they met Jackson and Bass, who had just returned from Dallas County, and went with them to camp. They remained in the camp a considerable time, and leaving Billie Collins there, returned to Denton without having come to any definite agreement. Tom Gerren, one of Eagan's deputies, had once been in the camp too, remaining but a little time, during which he was under the cover of "Arkansaw" Johnson's cocked Winchester.

Will Scott, who had been a deputy sheriff of Dallas County, knowing of the large rewards offered for the capture of Bass, conceived in the winter of 1877-78 the idea of capturing Bass, if possible. He knew that Bass had been with Joel Collins, and he reasoned that Bass, after his arrival in Texas, would hold some sort of communication with the Collins boys, Billie and Henry, brothers of Joel, and he thought the best plan he could adopt to gain the confidence of Bass would be through them. To this end he began cultivating the Collins boys, with whom he was very well acquainted, until finally he induced Billie to go with him to Bass's camp in Denton County, about the last of March or first of April, and he remained there with Collins a day or two. The efforts and services of Scott will be given in detail in another chapter.

In the meantime there had been such a clamor in the public press about northern Texas that Governor Hubburd had taken action and sent Major John B. Jones, of the Frontier Battalion, to Dallas to inquire into matters, and to recruit a company of Rangers for service against the bandits, if in his judgment he thought it advisable. Major Jones consulted with Captain June Peak, and learned from him the nature of the country in which the robbers had their retreat, and learned from Will Scott what he knew about them and their stronghold. So he commissioned June Peak as a lieutenant in the Frontier Battalion and instructed him to recruit twenty men for the service. Captain Peak soon had all the men he wanted and went into camp near Dallas.

The first service done by Peak and his Rangers was to go and arrest Pipes and Herndon, but of this we will speak in another chapter.

CHAPTER XII

Opening of the Campaign

*Various arrests—Hard work in the saddle—A good deal
of gunpowder burned—Bass proves himself to
be a wily fox and an adroit general*

THE CAMPAIGN, for we don't know how better to term
it, commenced in good earnest against Bass and his
outlaws during April, say the 24th or 25th of the month.
On the 13th of April, General Walter P. Lane, deputy
United States marshal, was in Denton, and made affidavits against Sam Bass, Frank Jackson, Henry Underwood,
"Arkansaw" Johnson, and Seaborn Barnes, charging them
with stopping the train and robbing the United States
mail, before United States Commissioner Alexander
Robertson, who issued warrants for their arrest and put
them in the hands of Sheriff Eagan. In the meantime,
Will Scott was still at work trying to entrap Bass, and
even after the arrest of Pipes and Herndon, he went up
into Denton County and met Bass at Green Hill's house.
There they agreed to rob the bank of Gaston and Thomas,
in Dallas, and Scott left for Dallas to complete the
arrangements for the raid, the details of which were partly
mapped out. While Scott was in Dallas, Billie Collins
wrote to Bass to hang Will Scott to the nearest tree the
next chance he had, for Scott was a spy and a traitor.
Collins had become satisfied that Scott had given Pipes

97

and Herndon away, and this letter he sent by Scott Mayes
to Bass. Scott wanted to return to Bass's camp and lead
him into the trap of robbing the bank, feeling satisfied
that he could allay any suspicions Collins' letter might
have aroused, but Major Jones, of the Frontier Battalion,
would not consent; besides, he was averse to trying the
bank robbery scheme for fear someone would get hurt,
as the robbers were desperate men.

The federal court was in session at Tyler at this time,
and on the evidence Captain June Peak had secured
through Will Scott, and on his own trip through the Cross
Timbers, and otherwise, indictments were found against
Green Hill, Monroe Hill, Henderson Murphy, Jim
Murphy, Scott Mayes, Wm. Miner, Riley Wetzel, Bill
Scaggs, a Negro, and a lawyer living at Denton named
Mullin, since dead, a relative of the Collins boys, and
they were all at different times arrested and carried to
Tyler, where they gave bond. The charges against these
men were for being accessories to the robberies. We will
speak of their cases further on.

About the date given before, the 24th or 25th of April,
the Rangers, under command of Lieutenant June Peak,
went into the Cross Timbers below Bass's principal
stamping grounds. Sheriff Wm. Everheart, of Grayson
County, with a few men from Captain Lee Hall's company of state policemen, and a small posse of citizens,
entered the Cross Timbers above the Bass headquarters,
and Sheriff Eagan, of Denton County, with some of his
deputies and a posse of citizens, advanced on the front
direct to the robber stronghold. Thus it will be seen that
Captain Bass and company were not only flanked on the
right and left, but had a force directly in his front and
escape would seem almost a miracle. The woods were full

of armed men determined on the capture or death of the bold train raiders, and the cordon they had formed gradually began to close in. Sheriff Eagan was the first one to flush the game. Only a few miles from the town of Denton he met in battle array the bold Bass, his whilom man servant, his erstwhile trusted teamster, who had been a member of his family, who had spent months in his household, an honest, sober, industrious man, and who could still have been the same, but for his having forsaken the paths of honesty to become an outlaw, an Ishmael with his hand raised against all men, and the hands of all men now raised against him.

It was but a little skirmish Sheriff Eagan had with him, but the echoes of the rifle shots reverberated throughout all North Texas, the entire state, in fact, and even flashed along the telegraph wires, notifying all the land that the officers of the law were pressing hard after Bass and his train robbers. Railroad officials smiled with delight, the officers and messengers of express companies were rejoiced, United States postal route agents felt easier, and the traveling public breathed freer, for apprehensions of further train robberies vanished.

The great trouble that manifested itself now was the absence of an acknowledged head and leader for the forces of the law in pursuit of Bass. There was no concert of action, each party acting independent of the other and upon its own volition. The consequence was that there was constant riding to and fro in the Cross Timbers without effect. Bass knew the forces were after him, and he was always on the alert. A great many people in the Cross Timbers had been recipients of kindnesses at his hands, and besides they were helpless against him and his band, their lives and property being at his mercy, and they could not refuse to supply his necessities, nor give him intimations of danger when he called upon them. It was at this juncture in his affairs, with fate frowning upon him and seemingly holding above his head another sword of Damocles, that "Arkansaw" Johnson advised Bass to leave the country and escape the officers. He wanted the whole gang to slip off quietly to Arkansas and rob a bank or two, and then make their way to Mexico, where they could settle down in peace and safety, but Bass would not listen to him. All his resentment was aroused, the spirit of contention and defiance was big in him, and he determined to brave it out, believing that he could hold his ground against all the force they could bring against him in the Cross Timbers, and such was his personal magnetism and influence with his men that they determined to stay with him.

The next encounter with the robbers was on Sunday, April 29th. Bass and his gang were at the house of Jim Murphy when they discovered Sheriff Everheart and his party advancing toward the house. Cove Hollow, a deep canyon covered with dense timber on its either side, and with steep, precipitous bluffs, impassable in many places, was between Everheart and his posse and Murphy's house. Bass and his gang immediately left the house, mounted their horses, and advancing to the edge of the canyon, prepared to give Everheart battle. Bass called out to Everheart and his party, "Hell! Stand up and fight like men; don't be dodging 'round!" He then immediately fired at Everheart. With this both parties commenced firing, and the crack of rifles and six-shooters sounded like fun on a skirmish line during the late war. The width of the canyon at this point was about five hundred yards, and Sergeant Parrot, of Hall's state police, being an expert at long range, took as good aim at Bass as he could with Bass in motion and firing, shot away his cartridges and belt. Firing at him a second time, he struck the breech of Bass's Spencer rifle, the splinters flying in his face. At this Bass said, "Hell! boys, they've hit me at last. Let's get away from here." Sheriff Everheart and his party could not cross the canyon at this point, so they were forced to look at the robbers galloping off into the timbers without being able to give chase.

The robbers rode on at an easy pace, after galloping half a mile, to Henry Underwood's house, and giving Mrs. Underwood $100 they rode on a few miles, and then doubling on their trail returned to Underwood's house, where they kept a lookout for Everheart with a field glass Bass had, for a few hours, then they again took the saddle and plunged into the depths of the Cross Timbers, with every cow path and hog trail of which they were perfectly familiar, being able to tell their exact whereabouts any time day or night. Riding on they were espied by Deputy Sheriff W. R. Wetzel and Constable A. R. McGintie, who were traveling the road north of Bolivar, a little hamlet thirteen miles from Denton and near Cove Hollow.

The robbers, seeing Wetzel and McGintie, fled in a gallop, going in an easterly direction. Wetzel and McGintie pursued them until dark came on. The next morning, with Captain Whitehead, a farmer with whom they had spent the night, they took up the trail on foot, the undergrowth and timber being too dense for horseback travel. They followed the trail to the back of Captain Whitehead's plantation in Clear Creek bottom to the camp of the robbers, coming in sight of them just as they were leaving after their breakfast. They followed them, trailing them on foot, with the hopes of coming up with them at a halt, as they did not know they were being pursued, as far as Clear Creek, when Captain Whitehead, giving out, returned home. Wetzel and McGintie separated, each following a trail, until they passed out of the morasses and thickets of Clear Creek on the prairie which extended for miles on either side of the creek. On the prairie, Wetzel and McGintie met and continued on the trail until about eight o'clock A.M., when they discovered the robbers in camp on Hard Carter's place, four and a half miles from the town of Denton.

Wetzel sent word to Eagan that he had the robbers treed, and that officer at once summoned a posse of five men, Alex Cockrell, of Dallas, being one of the number, and hastened to the spot. Eagan deployed his men under cover of the timber and had the brigands completely surrounded, as he thought. Wetzel went up to Carter's house to reconnoitre and discovered the robbers eating their breakfast about 150 yards from Carter's house. Carter was at home, and while Wetzel was talking to him, he was seen by Bass and his gang, who at once sprang to their horses and commenced to saddle them, and as soon as they could, they mounted and broke off in a run in the direction they had come. Bass exclaimed, "To Clear Creek bottom, boys!" Wetzel fired a signal shot, and dismounting took position near the path they had run off and opened fire upon them. Captain Whitehead, who had returned home and got his horse, Jack Yates, and Finley Grisson also dismounted and opened fire on them as they ran off. By this time all Eagan's posse had closed in and joined in the melee and a running fight ensued, the robbers yelling and firing back at their pursuers. Eagan and his men pressed them hard, following them into the woods near the house of a man named Etters, where the robbers dodged them under cover of the timber, and making a circuit, came in behind them and then struck off south-eastward for the bottom of the Elm Fork of the Trinity River. The robbers dropped several blankets, an overcoat or two, along with some of their cooking utensils, but no one was hurt on either side.

The news soon spread that Eagan was fighting the robbers, and the greatest excitement prevailed in Denton. By night fifty men, armed with whatever they could get, were on the trail. Eagan returned to town to organize the forces rapidly volunteering to assist him in capturing the robbers, and the next morning, Tuesday, May 2d, the woods were full of men. Monday night the men divided into two squads, one under the command of Tom Yates running into the robbers, whom in the darkness they did not know until it was too late. The next morning this squad effected a junction with Lieutenant June Peak and his Rangers, and on foot they followed the trail of the robbers through the morasses and jungles of Elm bottom until they scattered.

The robbers were concealed in some of the almost impregnable fastness between Elm Fork and Hickory Creek, both these streams having wide, dense bottoms, with the high land between covered with a heavy growth of timber and underbrush. The robbers were perfectly familiar with the entire section. They knew every trail or path through the bottoms or highlands and thus had greatly the advantage of their pursuers. Besides this, the few people who lived amid these woods were mostly friends of the robbers, who would not only supply their wants, but would give them information as to the movements of those endeavoring to apprehend them.

By 10 o'clock on Tuesday morning, May 2d, there were

not less than 150 citizens of Denton County, under command of Sheriff Eagan, besides Lieutenant Peak's detachment of state Rangers, and Sheriff Everheart's posse, in the northern portion of the county. These men were scattered through the swamps of Elm Fork and Hickory Creek and the woods between and driving them toward June Peak's Rangers, who were coming up, meeting Eagan's posse. It seemed almost an impossibility for the robbers to escape and but for their superior knowledge of the country, they could not have done so.

A squad of Eagan's posse under command of Hon. Thos. E. Hogg, county judge of Denton County, were the first ones to find the robbers. A countryman met them and told them he could show them the fresh trail of horses entering Hickory Creek bottom, and going to the spot, Judge Hogg and his party took the trail, having to follow it on foot, the jungle and undergrowth being too thick to ride. They followed this trail on through the bottom and across the creek, having in the meantime notified Eagan, who with his forces also took to the bottom, until they finally came in sight of one of the robbers, who they took for Underwood. The robber fled hurriedly at their approach, but they kept up the pursuit until they came upon the whole party in camp eating their breakfast. The robbers fled, leaving their cooking utensils and two of their horses, one belonging to Bass and the other to Frank Jackson. Judge Hogg took the animal belonging to Jackson, and I. D. Ferguson the one belonging to Bass. The pursuers felt sure of a capture now, as two of the gang were afoot, but they counted without their host. Although the woods and bottoms were scoured thoroughly and closely, Bass was adroit enough to lead his men out of the trap. Near Warner Jackson's house, a brother to Frank

Jackson, a fine shawl was found hanging to a limb which contained a bucket full of cooked victuals of the very best kind, warm from the stove, which made the second breakfast the bandits were cheated out of. Two or three collisions took place during the day between different squads in the pursuit mistaking each other for the robbers. In one of these Deputy Sheriff Tom Gerren and party charged some of Peak's Rangers and John Work fired on them. Peak's men were just about to return the fire when they discovered that they were not the robbers.

It being impossible to find the trail or come across the robbers themselves, the bulk of the pursuing party returned to their home, though Peak and Eagan continued the hunt. As nothing could be seen or heard of the robbers, it was supposed they had fled the country and gone to Mexico, though Eagan and Peak followed what they thought was a trail of the robbers to Jack County. The robbers had not, however, left Denton County. They had simply kept in hiding in the ravines and swamps of Hickory Creek, and several times parties hunting for them passed in a few yards of them. On one of these occasions Sheriff Eagan and Judge Hogg went so close to the robbers that Bass took deadly aim at Eagan, and Jackson at Hogg, determined to fire if they were discovered, but as good fortune would have it, neither of these gentlemen saw them and were consequently permitted to pass on.

CHAPTER XIII

The Robber Campaign Goes On

The pursuit in Stephens County—They purchase provisions and leave a defiance for their pursuers—They take in a party of farmers—They return to Denton County

O N THE 7th of May, as the excitement seemed to have subsided and there was no one on the hunt for them in Denton County, the robbers ventured out of their hiding place and struck a bee line for Stephens County, about one hundred miles southeast from Denton. The first thing heard of them was through a telegraph dispatch from Fort Griffin, in Shackleford County, which read as follows: "Sam Bass and five of his men are surrounded in Big Caddo Creek, by Berry Meadows, sheriff of Stephens County. Meadows was re-enforced by ten men from Palo Pinto last night at 2 o'clock. He expected to make an attack at daylight next morning. Some fighting was done yesterday and the day before. No damage was done on our side. It is not known whether the outlaws were hurt."

The *Fort Worth Democrat,* then a daily paper, gave the following narrative of the Big Caddo Creek encounter, and as it is an accurate statement of affairs, we produce it. The Democrat said:

"Deputy Sheriff Freeman was informed last week by a woman of the neighborhood, near Caddo Creek, that parties answering the description of the train robbers were there. He, with one Ranger, and Messrs. Amis and Paschall of this town, went into that section to ascertain something more definite, and learned that Bass, Underwood, Jackson, Barnes, and two others, supposed to be Welch and Collins (Henry Collins had joined the band sometime previous to this), had been camped there in the mountains for upward of two weeks. A brother-in-law of Jackson, and several other kin and friends are living near Caddo Creek, and had furnished them with supplies. They are reported to be flush with twenty dollar gold pieces, and from events developed more recently, they are found to have numerous friends in that vicinity. Having gathered the desired information, the Ranger reported to his camp in Shackleford County, and the balance reported to Breckenridge, where Sheriff Meadows and Deputies Freeman and Hood selected several picked men, and on Sunday started for the scene of action. At midnight they sent back for re-enforcements, and twenty old shot guns were collected together and the same number of volunteers. Before all of these new recruits arrived, the sheriff's posse came upon the gang near the store thirteen miles east of here, on the Palo Pinto road, and an engagement ensued, in which about forty shots were fired by each party, and at one time three of the party dismounted and fought from behind trees. It is thought one of their horses was wounded. They afterward chased the robbers about two miles into the mountains. As the gang was so much better armed than the sheriff's party, and were acquainted with the locality of the mountain defiles, they then had little to fear. On Monday night they camped among the trees and thickets near Taylor's store, and the sheriff's party on the prairie one-half mile distant.

"Tuesday morning, May 26th, the sheriff and his posse

were gladdened by the arrival of the gallant Rangers from Shackleford County, nineteen in number, armed to the teeth, and their force had also been increased by Deputy Sheriff Owen and eight picked men from Palo Pinto town. The Rangers were under command of Lieutenant Campbell and Sergeant Jack Smith, and the Breckenridge party under Deputy Sheriff Freeman. Sergeant Smith, of the Rangers, stated that if they could find them, they would capture the robbers dead or alive, if they lost half of their men in the attempt. On Tuesday they followed their trail through the mountain gaps and defiles, and among the hills and valleys in their winding course, but up to twelve o'clock last night had not overtaken them, though the gang had come back to near the starting point. At McClasen's store, four miles further east, they purchased eight dollars worth of provisions, and left word for their pursuers that they would stand their ground and give them a desperate fight, and that they did not intend to be bulldozed, all of which is supposed to be a blind, and that they in reality were preparing to strike out for parts unknown. It was ascertained that they had been trying to swap off one of their horses. They are said to be well armed with a Winchester and a pair of six-shooters. Before the arrival of the Rangers the sheriff had summoned four or five citizens in that neighborhood to secure arms and join his posse.

"The Bass gang passed the same party soon after, before they had obtained arms, and marched them down to the store and treated them to bottled beer. It is said that parties in that vicinity have carried Bass's gang basketsful of provisions and kept them informed of the movements of their pursuers. One of the gang, it is reported, is suffering from a wound received in Denton. One of them remarked to some persons at the store that they were no petty thieves, that they interfered with no private citizen, but, holding out a handful of twenty dollar gold pieces, 'that is what the sheriff and his posse want.'

"They are said to have $5,000 with them and buried the balance. In getting volunteers from Breckenridge, it was quite manifest that a great portion of the citizens considered it their duty to join the home guard, and gallantly paraded the streets in their vigilance to find Sam Bass whom they proposed to demolish forthwith.

"The Rangers from Coleman County are expected across the country, to intercept them in case of a retreat in that direction. Additional parties from Griffin passed here last night to join the forces and aid in the capture."

But despite all these preparations and marshaling of men, Sam Bass escaped his pursuers and outgeneraled them in the cedar breaks and rocky hollows of the mountains.

These robbers, despite the perils they were in, had a keen eye to the ridiculous and were well disposed to have a little innocent fun when the occasion offered. Four farmers, their souls longing within them for glory, put on their war-paint, armed themselves with shot guns, and started out on the wild hunt for Bass and his gang. As they were riding along the road going in the direction the robbers were last heard from, they came up with a squad of men, well mounted and well armed, whom they took to be Rangers. They immediately inquired for the robbers and were anxious for directions whereby they could find them at once. They were tired of so much riding backward and forward and fuss being being made about the arrest of four or five robbers, and they proposed to put a stop to it by "taking the gang in out of the wet" just as soon as they came up with them. Bass and his men listened to them, smiling, until they finished their rhodomontade, and then in the twinkling of an eye the farmers found seven six-shooters flashed in their faces with the order to throw up their hands, and up their hands went, like they had been so many jumping jacks with somebody pulling the string. They were then disarmed by the robbers and marched up to Taylor's store, where the boys had lots of fun at their expense and wound up by making them all "boiling drunk" and then returning their arms to them with the admonition to go home and stay there, for if they were found by them hunting Bass and his gang any more, they would shoot them on sight, and these warlike farmers retired to the privacy of their own homes, where they remained during the rest of the campaign.

After dodging around at their leisure in the cedar breaks and mountain gorges in Stephens County, and being surrounded by posses watching their supposed avenues of escape, several times as reports had them, they whipped around, and dodged back into Denton County.

CHAPTER XIV

Efforts to Capture the
Robbers Continued

*The most daring feat of the robbers—They enter the town
of Denton by night and recapture the horses they had
lost—The indignant officers pursue them but in vain
—The Salt Creek fight, and death of "Arkansaw"
Johnson—A Dallas County Ranger fires the
deadly missle—Three more of the gang here
leave Captain Bass to return no more*

B ASS NOR any of his gang had been in Denton County
since May 7th, and nearly a month having elapsed,
the people were congratulating themselves upon the
riddance. The good name of Denton County had suffered
because of the presence of these outlaws within her confines, and the good people of the county were sore under
the animadversions of the press and public, and they were
rejoiced that if they had not been able to capture the
rascals and hand them over to that justice they deserved,
they at least aided materially in driving them out of the
country.

They were just beginning to feel easy and breathe
freely, when on June 5th, Bass and his men suddenly made

their reappearance in Denton County. The first seen of them was at the house of a man named Henry Crystal, a relative by marriage to Henry *[one or more words indecipherable in original]* with Bass, to whom they appealed for provisions. Crystal refused them peremptorily, telling them he would give them no countenance nor aid of any kind, and they at once left his house.

He immediately notified his neighbors of the presence of the robbers in the community, and they forthwith sent a courier to Elizabethtown, a hamlet not far distant, to notify Sheriff P. C. Withers who was at that point, and he at once summoned a posse and repaired to the scene where the robbers were last known to be, arriving there after night. He hastened a courier on to Sheriff Eagan in Denton, but the courier lost his way in the dark and did not get to Denton before nine o'clock the next morning, before which time the entire populace had been made painfully aware of the presence of Captain Bass and his gang.

When Bass and his men left Crystal's house, they wound around through the woods and bottoms, keeping out of sight of habitations, and gradually working their way nearer to the town of Denton. They were on a mission which for boldness and audacity was to surpass any of their feats. Camping for the night near town, they on the morning of June 6th, about six o'clock, dashed into Denton, but few people being up at that time of the day to see them, and going to the front of Work's livery stable, Bass and Jackson dismounted and entered the stable while Underwood, Johnson, and Collins remained at the door on guard. On getting inside of the stable, Bass and Jackson demanded of Charles McDonald, the stable keeper, the two horses that had been captured from them a few weeks before, and that were kept in the stable. McDonald hesitated about complying with their demand when Jackson struck him a heavy blow over the head with his six-shooter, but Bass interfered to prevent violence and made two of the hostlers bring out the horses and put on them the first saddles they came to, when the party left in a gallop. As they rode off, Underwood laughed one of his hearty peals, exclaiming: "Damn 'em, we'll show 'em they can't steal anything from us that we can't get back."

In a room over the stable, John Work and another man were asleep, but by the time they awoke and realized what was going on, the robbers had gotten away. They, however, spread the news over town at once, and in a little while Sheriff Eagan had a posse and was in full chase. On the prairie the trail was lost, but about three miles from Denton, Eagan and three of his posse came in sight of them, where they had stopped, but they soon disappeared in Clear Creek bottom.

About this time Charlie Carter, a young man whose father lived near Denton, joined the robbers. Young Carter was in rather bad odor, with some indictments hanging over him in Denton perhaps, and besides he knew that it was known that he had been in Bass's camp and had associated with him and his marauders a good deal, and being apprehensive of arrest on a capias from the United States court, especially as he saw so many people being taken up to that court at Tyler, he joined the robber band for protection.

Eagan and his men were now in earnest and fully determined on the capture of the bandits if human agencies, pluck, and energy could compass the end. The chase opened lively and in earnest. The pursuers stopped for nothing and gave the pursued no chance to rest.

After the robbers entered Clear Creek bottom, they were seen no more until the next morning, the 7th, though their trail was followed all the time. When caught sight of they were near Pilot Knob, six miles southeast of Denton, they were purchasing some provisions at the Knob, and having in their possession a fine horse they had stolen the night before near the town of Denton.

The appearance of the robbers in this vicinity put the people on the *qui vive*. Intense excitement ensued, and every man who could get a gun or a horse fit to ride joined pell mell in the chase. P. C. Withers and T. M. Yates, deputy sheriffs, with a posse of men had been sent early in the morning to find the trail, and striking it near Denton, followed them to Pilot Knob, where they came up with them, a skirmish ensuing. The robbers did not stand their ground long, but they succeeded in giving Geo. W. Smith, marshal of Denton, a flesh wound in the thigh which necessitated his return home.

Withers started couriers at once to Denton and Elizabeth-town for re-enforcements, but one of these couriers, a young man named Martin, was captured by the robbers. He was riding a mule which they took from him, turning it loose on the prairie after cutting his reins and appropriating the saddle. They not only left him afoot, but they robbed him of what money he had with him, and this was done, too, with their pursuers riding down upon them at a breakneck pace.

The robbers then made for the timber and concealing themselves waited until P. C. Withers, who was in advance of his posse, came suddenly upon them, when they fired a volley upon him and again retreated. Sheriff Eagan and his posse had by this time hurried and joined in the chase. He followed their trail about a mile when the robbers again concealed themselves. They suffered the posse to pass them and doubtless would have let them gone on, only they were discovered by two of the posse, Jesse Chinn and Giles Hammett, just after they had ridden by them. Chinn called out to Eagan that they were there, when they fired on Chinn and Hammett. It seemed miraculous that the miscreants killed no one, for they were all good shots and all had nerve enough to shoot with steady hands, but fate seemed to befriend the pursuers.

As soon as they had fired their volley, they broke to run again, doubling back the way they had come from, and crossing their trail made for Bullard's Mill, an easterly direction. For two miles and a half the chase was nip and tuck until finally they were overtaken in a little prairie, and a running, rattling fight ensued for a mile and a half without anyone being hurt. Withers and Wetzel led the pursuers and at times were as near as thirty or forty steps of the robbers, but could not shoot one of them.

By this time the robbers found Withers and Wetzel and Eagan meant serious business and they put their horses down to solid flight, and being better mounted than those who were after them, they set out in earnest to escape. The ground was soft, however, from recent rains, and there was no trouble in tracing their footsteps as they sped along through bramble and break and over stones and hollows. Through the Cross Timbers they took their course, and on that hot June day, the thermometer mounting to nearly a hundred degrees, it was the warmest sort of work for the horses and riders as well, but their pursuers never flagged, albeit their horses were panting and foam flecked.

During the entire day the robbers kept up their flight with the sleuth hounds of justice at their heels. Not less than seventy-five miles were traveled in this retreat and pursuit, and several times the leaden messengers of death hurtled about the heads of pursued and pursuers. Tom Gerren and Riley Wetzel, both deputy sheriffs of Denton County, accidently became separated from the other pursuers in making a detour, and after riding on for some little time, mistook the posse they had left for the robbers and opened fire upon them, which being vigorously returned, Wetzel was wounded painfully in the calf of the leg, he being the second man of the pursuers wounded during the course of the day.

At Davenport's Mills, a small hamlet beyond Denton Creek, the robbers stopped for a few moments, Bass going into the store of a man named Harvey Throope to purchase some provisions. At the time Throope was waiting on some ladies and informed Bass that he would attend to his wants in a few minutes. Bass replied with an oath, "Look here! I am in a hurry and I want you to wait on me! I am Sam Bass!" "Certainly, sir, certainly," said Throope, "Excuse me, ladies!" And he immediately gave his most courteous attention to the bandit, who paid for his purchases and hurriedly left.

Eagan and his party followed the robbers so closely as to force them across Denton Creek, and at 10 o'clock that night they camped on their trail. The next morning a mile from their camp they found where the robbers had stopped and eaten some canned fruits and meats, and about a mile beyond this the bandits scattered. At Elizabeth-town, Sheriff Eagan had secured the services of two men named Medlin and Stein, both old Indian fighters and frontiersmen, as trailers, and such was the skill of these men that they were able to follow the robbers in a gallop never once losing trace of their course. When they reached the point where the robbers had scattered, they took one trail and following it about a mile found where all the trails came together again. This separation was a cute trick of the robbers to gain distance on their pursuers. They expected the force following them to be bewildered by the number of trails going in different directions, and reasoned that they would stop and consult, but in this they were deceived, as the trailers, Medlin and Stein, never hesitated or halted but kept straight on, following the plainest defined trail.

Five miles further on, the bottoms and ravines of Hickory Creek were reached, near to and a little south of the robbers' old camp in that fastness. Following on as best they could through the dense brush and chapparal and hollows of the bottom, they suddenly ran upon the robbers at breakfast just back of the field of Warner Jackson, a brother of Frank. The pursuers were within sixty yards of the robbers before either of the parties spied the other, when the robbers discharged a volley with their Winchesters, killing two horses of Eagan's party belonging to Work Brothers, livery men in Denton, and ridden by Alex Cockrell and John Work. Their fire was returned with interest, and for a few moments a brisk fight ensued, the sheriff's posse pressing forward until the robbers broke and fled, being so closely followed that Underwood's horse, all the camp equipage, their breakfast, the coffee still smoking hot on the fire, all their provisions, and the saddle taken from the courier Martin, the day before, were captured. Underwood mounting behind one of the other robbers, the two rode double until they came to the house of Reuben Bandy, a quarter of a mile distant, when Underwood took the pony of John Hyatt, tied to the fence, telling Hyatt as he galloped off that he wanted to borrow the pony a little while.

117

They passed on back of the field of a man named Hicks and crossing Hickory Creek continued in a northerly direction, passing in about five miles of the town of Denton and heading straight for Clear Creek. They had been under whip and spur, pursued and pursuers, the better part of two days, had traveled near a hundred miles, two men had been wounded, two horses killed, and the robbers forced to abandon some of their possessions, and yet at no time had they been exceeding fifteen miles from the town of Denton.

Before the bandits crossed Hickory Creek, the trail was lost, that of some other squad of pursuers being taken for it, but in about three hours it was found again. In the meantime the town of Denton was all aglow with excitement. It looked like a tocsin of war had sounded and that every man in the community had suddenly responded. There was mounting in hot haste and the seizing of arms, for the crowd divined the way the robbers would take and were anxious to head them off, if possible, from the swamplands of Clear Creek.

A party under command of Captain Grady entered the bottom of the Elm Fork of the Trinity River, near the crossing of that stream known as the Fishtrap, and forcing their way up the stream to where Clear Creek debouches into it, went up that creek to the Pilot Point road, but there could find no trace of the bandits. Eagan and his posse lost the trail after they struck the McKinney road, and as the most of them had had not exceeding one meal for themselves or horses and no rest for the better part of two days, they separated into squads and went in search of provisions and provender.

After the parties had separated, Deputy Sheriff John Carroll of Denton County, Jim Courtwright, marshal of

Fort Worth, Bill Woody, a policeman of the same place, and Jack Yates, deputy sheriff of Denton County, came upon the robbers accidently about sundown and chased them into Elm bottom, where they lost them.

The next morning about daylight they were seen at the little village of Bolivar, Bass having during the previous night remounted his whole party on fresh, fine horses. At Bolivar they bought five hundred rounds of ammunition and $50 worth of provisions. At this time Sheriff Everheart of Grayson County, United States Deputy Marshal Johnson of Sherman, and Deputy Sheriff Parish of Cook County, had started out to join in the effort to capture the robbers. Eagan, hearing of the gang at Bolivar, got his posse together again and repaired immediately to that point to find that the birds had flown.

About 12 o'clock that day, Monday the 8th, Everheart, Johnson, and Parish, with their men, found the robbers in camp just preparing to eat. They had just sweetened their coffee when their pursuers rode upon them, and they dashed at once for their horses, leaving everything behind them but their horses. It was a stampede from that point on to Clear Creek, a stretch of about twelve miles. With the robbers it was a life and death matter, and John Gilpin never rode a wilder race. Everheart and his men were fast at their heels firing on them at every jump and never were such a twelve miles made in quicker time or under more exciting circumstances than were these. But for the fact that the robbers had the night before provided themselves with fresh horses, they would inevitably have been captured or "wiped out."

Finally the robbers reached the hills bordering on Clear Creek, where it seemed that nothing but a chamois could make headway, but Bass and his thieves never stopped to think of this, but plunging madly down a precipice which to look at was enough to make one shudder, they disappeared in the dense woods at the foot. Everheart and his party were at the spot where they went over, and down seemingly to certain death, but they did not care to peril life and limb in that way, so they sought and found a better point of getting into the swamp, during which time the robbers escaped them and made their way across the prairie beyond.

June Peak and his state Rangers had not been idle all this time, but on the contrary had been on the warpath the most of the time following the Simmons trail of the robbers with that unerring precision that always finds its prey. He had with him as trailer, a frontiersman who buffalo hunted for a living when he wasn't after Indians, in the service of the government as a scout, known as "Buffalo Bill," not the original of that name, though a man somewhat after his character, but without his general intelligence or refinement. This "trailer" was leading the Rangers straight to the robbers, when the boys were overtaken by John Carroll, a deputy sheriff of Denton County, Mr. Stoker, deputy sheriff of Tarrant County, and W. P. Withers, they having become separated from Eagan's posse. Sheriff Stephens, of Wise County, with a posse of men, also joined them in the pursuit.

After leaving Clear Creek, the robbers had ridden straight across the country into Wise County until they struck the timbers of Salt Creek, and entering into the heart of the bottom, they turned up the creek, winding around among and threading their way through the jungles and breaks. Peak and his men were close behind them and followed slowly and cautiously the trail, hoping to surprise them in camp, as they thought they had distanced pursuit for the time being.

Late in the afternoon the Rangers suddenly came upon them in camp under the trees on the bank of the stream, their horses being staked out near by.

This was a critical time. The Rangers and the posse with them were eager for the fray, and at the command of Lieutenant Peak, opened fire upon the outlaws. A sharp fight ensued and the most decisive one of the campaign, up to that time. The robbers had been hunted and run down from point to point until they had well nigh reached that point of desperation that they had as soon die as live and be badgered as they had been by pursuing parties who gave them no rest, no time to eat, and it seemed that they had determined to make a final stand at this point and let fate then and here decide the matter. They presented a bold front and returned shot for shot. "Arkansaw" Johnson stood out as coolly and unmoved as one of the trees beside him, firing indiscriminately, it seemed at first, until he singled out Sergeant Thomas A. Floyd, of the Rangers, and a duel with Winchester rifles took place between them. Floyd was a citizen of Dallas, a member of the Stonewall Greys, a volunteer military company of the city, and one of the company's rifle team and was a crack shot. To fight more effectually, he jumped from his horse, and dropping on his knee, took deliberate aim, fired, and "Arkansaw" Johnson sprang into the air a corpse, a rifle ball through his heart. The angel of death had hovered around him all that fateful day and with insatiate glee clutched his heart strings as Floyd's bullet sped its way, and launched his soul into eternity to render an account of the crimes he had committed, the murders, the outrages upon defenceless women, the robberies, the thefts, the blasphemies that he had piled up against himself.

Bass was standing by Johnson when he fell, and the sight of the dead face and staring eyes, full of the horrors of hell, that had opened up to him as the last convulsive breath left his body, seemed to unnerve the leader, and he fled precipitately, the rest of the gang slipping after him into the tangled undergrowth and crawling down under the bank of the creek, concealed themselves in a washout in the bank. While there, one of the Rangers looking for them came very near to them, and Frank Jackson drew a bead on him with his rifle, asking Bass if he must shoot, who replied, "No, not unless he turns this way."

Underwood from the opening of the engagement had given his attention to the horses, and reaching them had mounted one and carried the others off a short distance into a thick mote of timber, and was returning to take part in the fight when he was met face to face by Lieutenant June Peak. They began firing at each other simultaneously, but both being mounted, they could not take accurate aim and consequently did each other no harm. About the third fire apiece with their six-shooters Underwood wheeled his horse and ran, Peak after him, and shouting to his men to follow. He did not know the locality of the robbers, and seeing Underwood, presumed that he was a rear guard to cover their retreat, therefore he followed him and called for his men to come up. Proceeding a short distance in pursuit of Underwood, he saw the robbers' horses in the mote of timber, where Underwood had taken them, and at once he and his men began to "shell the woods," supposing the bandits to be where their horses were. The result was the killing of two horses and the capture of the rest. Diligent search was made for the robbers, but they could not be discovered, hidden as they were in their cave under the bank, until night coming on, the pursuers went into camp. Lieutenant Peak wanted to surround a dense thicket into which he believed the robbers had forced their way, but as he had not force enough himself and the posse under the command of Sheriff Stephens, of Wise County, would not act without his orders, and he had gone off after a coroner to hold an inquest on the body of Johnson, the proposition had to be abandoned.

During the night Bass and his men slipped out under cover of darkness, and stealing horses in the neighborhood, left for parts unknown.

The body of Johnson was turned over to citizens living nearby and was by them buried. Thus ended in blood and violence the life of one of the bravest, most reckless of the gang, a life that might have been of value to mankind had its energies been directed aright, and had noble purposes inspired him instead of evil propensities swaying him and leading him in all of his actions.

This fight virtually ended the campaigns against Bass and his bandits. It began April 24th, in Denton County, with a light skirmish and closed on Salt Creek, in Wise County, on June 12th, with the death of one of the robbers and their dispersion on foot. During the campaign four men were wounded, one man killed, four horses killed and a number captured, besides days and days and nights and nights of hard riding and peril. The robber band was reduced to three men by the Salt Creek fight, one from death and three others deserting them, namely, Henry Underwood, who was never seen by them again, he leaving for parts unknown, out of the country. His whereabouts have never been known, but it is believed that he is in Kentucky. His wife and children left Denton County shortly after he did, and it is said went to him in Kentucky. Charlie Carter also left them after this fight and returned to his father's house sick at heart, sore, and full of dread, sadder and wiser than he ever was before, truly repentant for all his violations of the law and longing that he might escape the difficulties that beset him. He lingered around his father's house hiding out in the woods and dodging the officers until finally he was taken sick and captured and taken to Austin for trial in the federal court. As he had never been with the Bass gang in any of their enterprises of stage aid railroad train robbery and was only connected with them after the campaign opened against them, he could only be charged with being an accessory after the fact, and as evidence was not to be had sufficiently positive of this, he was acquitted. He was subsequently arrested, however, on a capias from Cooke County, for horse stealing, and sent to the penitentiary, where he is now at hard labor along with an older brother, also in for horse stealing.

Henry Collins remained with Bass until they got down to Dallas County, when he, too, left him and returned to his father's mansion. We shall have more to say of Henry Collins in another chapter.

Before closing this chapter, let us indulge in a few reflections. Many people have wondered why, in an almost ceaseless campaign of seven weeks, with from fifty to one hundred men all the time, or nearly so, in hot pursuit of the robbers, they were not captured, especially as they were seen nearly every day. The only answer to this question is that in the section of country where the Bass gang had their headquaters, it was next to impossible to come up with or surround them. The growth of timber, briars, chapparal, and vines, and the lagoons and marshes were so thick and almost impenetrable that the robbers could with ease dodge their pursuers and keep out of their way. They were familiar with every niche in the ground, knew every hollow, thicket, and hiding place, and could follow every pig path and cow trail with unerring certainty, knowing exactly where it would take them, advantages their pursuers did not have. Furthermore, living in the Cross Timbers were a class of people, something on the order of squatters, who sympathized with the robbers, who befriended them in every way they could and acted as picket guards and spies, as it were, for them, giving them timely warning of the approach and locality of the officers of the law. All the people who lived in these woods were not of that kind, but a number were, as is well known. Another thing may seem strange—why were not some of the pursuers killed? Bass himself has answered that question. He did not want to shed blood; he wanted no man's life on his hands. He was simply a robber, making his money off the public, the rich corporations in the main, not a murderer, and it was his policy never to shed blood or allow it to be shed by any of his men when it could possibly be avoided. Many a time, he said, had his pursuers passed within ten feet of him and his men when he would be concealed in the thickets, and with their guns leveled on them they could have shot them down deliberately, but he did not desire to hurt them, except to protect himself.

The result of the campaign proved conclusively that if Captain June Peak's idea had been carried out, if his counsels could have prevailed, the ending would have been different. He had been through the country on horseback and afoot and he knew how great an advantage the outlaws would have in an open raid after them, therefore his tactics were to put up a job on them and lead them into ambush. Get them started on an expedition to carry into effect some scheme of robbery and thus draw them out of their stronghold, and while they were in the act of their crime, come down upon them with a superior force from all sides suddenly and force them to a surrender or else kill them. But so many sheriffs and deputy sheriffs and detectives and amateur officers of the law had become inspired with a greed for the rewards offered for Bass and the rest of his crowd that they must needs fill the woods with little posses armed with pot metal shot guns and mounted on spavined ponies to go chasing up and down the Cross Timbers shooting at one another, that there was never a chance to lead Bass into a trap. Mind is always superior to physical force, and what physical force, main strength and awkwardness failed to accomplish in seven weeks of hard service and danger, mind would have done in ten days had it been allowed to do so.

CHAPTER XV

Jim Murphy's Narrative

*Murphy joins the gang—They leave their old stomping
ground—On a wild hunt for a bank to rob—
Murphy leads them into a trap*

As STATED in a previous chapter, Jim Murphy, a cattle
man in Denton County, and his father, Henderson
Murphy, with a number of other persons in Denton
County, had been arrested under indictments found
against them in the United States Court at Tyler, and
had been taken to that place and bonded. They were to
appear and answer in June. The charge against these men
was for being accessories of Sam Bass and his gang in
their train and mail robberies. There is but little doubt
that Jim Murphy had a general knowledge of the acts of
Bass and his men, and after the facts perhaps had full
knowledge, and there would in all probability have been
evidence to convict. He was a personal friend of each one
of the robbers, he knew they were outlaws, his house was
open to any or all of them day or night, and he supplied
their wants whenever desired to do so. He knew that his
father, Henderson Murphy, was entirely innocent and he
felt that it was hard for an old man of irreproachable
character, who stood high for integrity and honesty with
everyone who knew him, like his father, to lay in a
dungeon, and he determined to do something to save his

father and himself. To this end he made a proposition to entrap Bass and his men if the charges against himself and his father were dismissed.

On the subject of the arrangement he made me give his own words as follows: "I, J. W. Murphy, was arrested May 1st, 1878, by Sheriff Everheart of Grayson County, for harboring Sam Bass. I was innocent of the charge and told Everheart so. I asked him why he did not tell me long ago that he wanted Bass. He gave me no answer of any satisfaction, but pushed me off from my family and put me in jail at Sherman. Walter Johnson took me from the Sherman jail and put me in jail at Tyler. On the way to the jail at Tyler I hinted the plan for capturing Sam Bass to Taylor and he said he would send Johnson to see me soon. Johnson came to see me after I had given bond. I told him I could plan a job to capture Sam Bass if I was foot loose. Johnson told me he would see me again soon. So he went off and came back with June Peak, and we talked the matter over. June says: 'I will go and see Major Jones.' The Major came and talked with me about the plan for the capture of Bass. At this time I made a contract with Major Jones as to what he would do for me and my father if I would catch Sam Bass. He said that if I would lay the plan for the capture of Sam Bass, that he would have my case and my father's dismissed, and that he would see that I should have my part of the reward and his part too. He said he did not want any of the reward, and that I should have what was right. I worked this plan under three men, Jones, Peak, and Johnson. Nobody else was to know anything about it. They were the men I relied on. After a short time Sheriff Everheart worked into the secret through Johnson. The first time that Everheart came to me I gave him no satisfaction.

128

The second time he came, a man by the name of Taylor was with him. Taylor told me that whatever Everheart told me would be all right with Johnson, and I let him into the secret against my own will."

When June Peak went to see Major Jones, they discussed the matter and agreed to accept the proposition if United States District Attorney Evans would agree to it, so they called on Judge Evans and imparting this plan to him, he gave his consent and the following written assurance of the same:

WHEREAS, James Murphy stands indicted as an accessory in robbing the United States mails, in several cases now pending in the United States District Court at Tyler, and, whereas, I believe public justice will be best subserved hereby, I, Andrew J. Evans, United States Attorney for the Western District of Texas, bind the United States as follows:

1st. If the said Murphy should leave Tyler, I will protect him and his bondsmen at this term of the court.

2d. If the said Murphy shall be instrumental in securing the arrest and delivery to the United States Marshal of the Western District of Texas, of all or any of the following principals, in their order (Bass, Jackson, Underwood, Barnes, and Johnson) in said indictments, then all prosecutions are to be dismissed as to said Murphy, growing out of his acts as accessory to the said principals; to be done upon the certificate of Major John B. Jones.

3d. In case Murphy shall use all reasonable and possible means in his power to capture the said Bass and his above named associates, and if Major John B. Jones will certify to such facts to the United States District Attorney, then the said Murphy is to have the relief named in section 2d above, although he may be unsuccessful.

(Signed) A. J. Evans
May 21st, 1878   U. S. Attorney

The cases against Henderson Murphy were then at once dismissed and he turned home. Jim hung around

Tyler a day or two and then jumped his bond, apparently, Lieutenant Peak aiding him to get out of town and borrowing the hat of a prominent attorney of Dallas who had been employed by the government to assist in the prosecution of the cases, while that attorney was out or asleep. Murphy's bondsmen were furious with him and in great worry at the idea of having to pay his bail bonds. They learned some way or other that June Peak had something to do with Murphy's running off, and they, suspecting him of improper motives, were disposed to raise a row about it. It was difficult to tell which raised the biggest row, the bondsmen left with a bag to hold or the lawyer whose hat was in the vocative. Finally, everybody was pacified, District Attorney Evans assuring the bondsmen that he would give them until the next term of the court before he would enter up judgment *nisi* against them on Murphy's bond, and Lieutenant Peak loaned the lawyer money enough to buy him a new hat. When Murphy reached Mineola, he had his huge red mustache shaved off, and with the lawyer's hat on, even his best friends would not have known him, so that he easily avoided rearrest, his bondsmen having telegraphed to Dallas that he be apprehended.

From the time of Murphy's departure from Tyler up to the fight at Round Rock we will give substantially in his own words, as it gives a full and succinct history of the actions of what was left of the gang up to that time, and throws some light on some things otherwise obscured. Murphy made this statement officially, shortly after the death of Bass. He said: "On the first of May, 1878, I was arrested and carried to Tyler. I jumped my bond after I had been there a few days, having made satisfactory arrangements to relieve myself and my father of our troubles, both of us being innocent of the charges preferred against us. I left Tyler secretly on the morning of May 22d, only District Attorney Evans, Major Jones, June Peak, Walter Johnson, and Sheriff Everheart knowing anything about it. I reached Denton the same night, and hiring a horse from Work Brothers, I started home. When I had gone about three miles from Denton, my horse ran into a barbed wire fence and threw me off, nearly breaking my neck. The horse ran off, kicking and pitching furiously. I was hurt so badly that I had to lay there until daylight next morning, when I got up and started home on foot. Meeting with a good friend on the way, I got into her buggy and went to my father's house, on the head of Hickory Creek. Here I mounted myself on a good horse, and went up to Wise County where my family was; and after staying there two days returned to Denton County, and stayed two weeks below Denton in the timber, between Hickory Creek and Elm, waiting for Bass and his gang to come in from Stephens County. Hearing of Bass fighting out there, and not knowing when he would come in, I left Hickory Bottom and went home, leaving word for Bass to come to my house when he returned, but Bass stopped at the town of Denton to recapture some horses that Sheriff Eagan's men had captured from him before. Bass got into such a hot fight over it that he could not get to my house, but started west, and had a fight with June Peak's Rangers and some citizens, on Salt Creek, where he lost a man called Arkansaw Johnson, but whose real name was Harlston; also losing his horses. Bass then turned back and came by Ft. Worth, and thence to Dallas, where the gang bought some pistols and came directly to my house on Cove Hollow, on the 15th of June, 1878. There was some company at my house and they did not stop, but rode by and made a sign by a lift of their hats so that I would come to them. As soon as I could excuse myself, I went to Bass and Jackson on the branch and met them. They shook hands with me and took on over me terribly. Bass said to me, 'Well old fellow how do you like to play checkers with your nose?' 'Not at all,' said I. 'That's nearly h——l, ain't it Jim?' said Bass. 'Well, old fellow, you had better come and go with me, and you won't have to play checkers with your nose. We have lots of fun and plenty of money in our camp.' 'Well,' I replied, 'I had thought of going with you boys, but I have about given it out and thought I would go back and stand my trial and come clear.' 'Yes, Jim, that's very nice, but you don't have any show with the United States, and with the prejudice there is against you. There is no showing for you boys, because they think you are friends of mine, and I tell you the best thing you can do is to go with me and make some money, and we will send the money back to pay the bond off as soon as we can make a strike.' I said: 'Well, Sam, if you will wait till I thresh my wheat tomorrow, maybe I'll go.' 'All right,' said Sam, 'if you will go, we will wait. We need you in our business.' So Sam gave me a $50 bill and told me to go up to Rosston and get some change for him which I did. They laid over until Monday, and I started with them. On Tuesday morning we went to Bolivar and got some ammunition and some baked bread. From this we went to Hickory Creek, near 'Lone Elm,' where we camped and stayed all night. Next morning we rose early. Bass said, 'Boys, we must get out from here to get breakfast.' So we saddled up and rode down the divide between the two Hickories, and wound into North Hickory back of Bob Carruth's field and got our breakfast in the bottom. We saw Carruth's hands plowing in the field. Sam said: 'If old Bob knew we were here wouldn't he raise h——l? But blast him, he don't know it.' Breakfast over, we started to find Billy Jackson's camp, for Frank wanted to trade horses with him. We went down Hickory Creek below the fork, and then went to 'Bush Knob,' as it was the highest point in this country. Bass said, 'We'll stay here a while and keep a look out for the herd.' While here Sam said to me, 'How are you on the shoot?' 'Not much,' I replied. 'Well, you had better practice, for I tell you that if 'Old Dad' (slang name for Sheriff Eagan) gets after us, you will have to shoot—for we mean business now, so let's practice a little right here.' Sam pointed out an object three or four hundred yards off and said, 'Now, boys, watch me hit that place. If that was old Judge Hogg, how easy I could bust his leather; I would make him wish that he had never straddled old Coly—the blamed old rascal. He ain't able to buy him a good horse, so he must step around and pick up my boys' horses. I took my gun down off of him once and wouldn't shoot him, but I will never do that any more.' We shot several times at different objects and Sam said I did very well. He then told me to always keep my arms in good fix for there was no telling when Dad Eagan might 'put up' and that that blasted Clay Withers is 'some h——l too, as you go along, but all we've got to do is to kill a few horses, then retreat and they'll kind o' go slow and won't crowd us much more. Well, boys, it's after 12 o'clock; we had better go back to the bottom and get dinner.'

"After dinner Sam sent me to the C 2 Ranche, to see if Billy Jackson was camped down there. I went and found Billy, and told him that Frank wanted to see him, and returned to Bass's camp, back of Carruth's field. We then all rode out on the ridge and stayed there all the evening. While we were there Guss Egan and Alonzo Carruth, two boys, came to us. Sam was mighty glad to see those two little boys, and said: 'Well, boys, I am looking out for a sheep ranche, and if these old grangers will let me alone, I will move in here, to be a neighbor to you, and go to raising sheep.' That tickled the boys, and they rode off laughing. As they rode off, Sam remarked: 'What would I give to be in their places! I would give all the gold I ever saw, and more too, if I had it. But it's too late now to think of that. I ought to have taken my father's advice when I was a little boy and shunned bad company; but h—ll, there is no use thinking about that now. It all goes in a lifetime, anyhow. I will make some old banker pay for my troubles; money will sweeten anything!' By this time it was nearly sunset. We went to Billy Jackson's camp and got supper. Frank Jackson said: 'Billy, I want Old Ben.' Billy said that he did not want to give him up. 'I am afraid that it will get me into trouble,' said he. 'Can't help it,' said Frank, 'I am bound to have him. Here's another in his place,' and he took the horse. Frank said, 'Jim, you had better get you another horse.' I went, then, and took my brother John Murphy's horse, and told him that he could take my horse back. John 'kicked' a little, and so did Billy. Sam said: 'Boys, it's no use to kick, for we must have good horses in our business.' We then mounted and went off laughing about how the boys kicked about a little thing. Sam said if they had ten thousand dollars he would pull them just to hear them squeal. We came on the Decatur road to Medlin's Point, about one mile and a half from Denton, when we rested until 12 o'clock, it being the intention to steal in the night a fine saddle-horse belonging to W. H. Mounts, in the suburbs of Denton. While here the boys told many fine stories about their adventures. Bass at length said: 'Well, boys, what do you reckon old Bill Mounts will say! I would like to be hid somewhere near, though I know what he will say as well as if I were there. The old rascal will walk out in the morning and find his horse and saddle gone. He will go back to the house with his lips hung down, and his face as long as h—ll. Well, old lady, my fine horse and saddle are gone. I just know that Sam Bass has got them. I wish I had never got that long-range gun. He said that he would make it cost me $10 every time I shot it. What shall I do! My horse is gone. I'll bet Jim Murphy told him about it. Jim, they'll give you h—ll over this thing; but that don't make any difference, for you have turned loose now anyhow.' I replied, 'That's all right; we'll just rob them all alike whenever we strike them.' 'That's the idea, Jim. That is what I have argued all the time. We had just as well rob one as another, for they are all after us, anyhow.'

"By this time it was about twelve o'clock. 'Let's be going, boys,' said Bass, 'we must pull Bill Mounts' horse.' So we mounted and rode to Mounts' house, stopping in front of his gate. I was left to guard while Sam went in and got a horse which he supposed to be Mounts', but it belonged to a traveler; he got Mounts' saddle. We then went east, passing through Denton, to Elm bottom, where we arrived just before sun-up. We were very tired, and stopped and slept about fifteen minutes. We then rode across Big Elm and stopped for breakfast, when we rested two or three hours. Seeing several men pass the road, Sam said, 'Boys, we'd better get away from here. Old Dad Eagan might be on our trail, and if he is, he will give us h—ll, for they are mad as h—ll. I guess we'll ride.' So we started east, and came to the bottom just above Lum Dickson's, then passed along the edge of the timber until we got below Hill Town, when we stopped and got dinner. As we rode on in the afternoon, we were all talking about the Rangers and grangers. Bass said: 'Now, boys, we'll quit this way of running. We are shut of Henry Underwood, and I hope we will stay shut of him, for he can't stand the racket, and I don't want any man with me that can't stand the racket. If I had never run from anybody, they never would have been so hot after me as they have been.' We then turned for Dallas County, passing through a large pasture, in a south-eastern course. It was a drizzly, dark evening, and we lost our way, and went to a farmer's house to stay all night. Sam said: 'Jim, you tell him we are hunting a pair of stolen mules and a big, fine horse; that we are Peak's Rangers, and that you live in Wise County, near Pelley, and that your name is Paine; that you met up with Captain Peak and got two of his Rangers to go with you to help arrest the thieves.' I told the old man the story the best I could. After supper Bass and the old farmer struck up a conversation about Bass. The farmer seemed to sympathize with Bass. He said he had heard that the railroads had beat Bass out of a large pile of money. Bass said he did not know anything about him. All he knew was that his captain, June Peak, had him out on several raids after him. It seemed like Bass must have some good traits about him, for he had lots of friends. The old man replied that he thought a heap of Bass himself, although he never saw him that he knew of. This tickled Bass mightily, and when we went upstairs to go to bed, Sam said, 'Well, it wouldn't take much to make this old man solid with me—he is old business!'

"Next morning we went east, passing the village of

Frankfort, in Dallas County. Here we got a horse shod, and Sam bought a lot of candy. While we were eating the candy, in came a poor farmer boy who had worked hard all the year and made nothing. He said he had a notion to go and hunt Bass and get with him and rob railroads and get some money, for he could not make any farming. This created quite a laugh in the little store. He then stepped up to Sam and said, 'Stranger, if you will give me some candy I will give you some peaches.' 'All right,' said Sam, and they traded.

"We made particular inquiry here about my fine mules, but did not hear of them. After we started away, Sam said: 'What do you reckon that fool would have said if I had told him that I was Bass, and have showed him a few twenties? I'll bet I could have broken his eyes off with a board! I'll bet he hasn't had twenty dollars this year. That is the way of the most of these old farmers. They never have any money. I had rather rob a train and have plenty of money. I never expect to work any more, unless it is before a shot-gun or something like that.' We stopped about two miles east of Frankfort to get dinner. While there old man Oby's mules and horses came around us playing. In the bunch was a mighty fine horse. Sam said, 'Old horse, you are a good one. Some of these times I will come around and pull you! Boys, don't you reckon old man Oby would kick if I did?'

" 'Yes; and I wouldn't blame him either,' said Jackson. 'It's too bad to take these old farmers' horses; it bothers them so bad!'

" 'H——l, h——l, h——l!' exclaimed Bass, 'what need I to care for their botheration; no skin off of my back! The dried old rascal is able to lose a good horse now and then. 'Let them kick; it don't amount to anything.' Sam then said we had better be riding, and we saddled and went on our way rejoicing. When we had gone a short distance, Bass said, 'Boys, you go ahead. I will turn off here and meet you again about two miles from here.' He rode off, and after awhile he overtook us in company with Henry Collins and two men I did not know. As they rode up, I heard one of the strangers say, 'Blast that Murphy! Sam you ought to go and kill him right now.' I did not hear any reply from Bass. I remarked to Jackson, 'Frank, do you hear that?' Jackson replied 'Yes, Jim, h——l is up! just be easy; I won't let them hurt you.' By this time they had reached us. They all seemed to be in a deep study, but said little. Bass said, 'Well, get upon your horses and we'll go over and get Sebe Barnes.' One of the new-comers said to Sam, 'They say they are looking for June Peak out here.' 'Yes, I feel like we are going to have h——l,' said Sam, in shrill, angry tones.

"When we started, one of the strangers said, 'Good-bye, boys; keep your eyes open and watch one another. I am afraid when I hear from you all again you will have h——l shot out of you.' He then rode away. Henry Collins and the other party went with us to where Sebe Barnes was. On the way there I saw that there was something wrong, and I said to Jackson, 'What is the matter with all the boys?' He replied that he didn't hardly know but guessed I would find out after a while. That scared me up, but I did not let on. Presently we came to a church in the edge of a bottom. I heard someone whistle, and asked what it was, and they said it was Sebe. Bass whistled then and Sebe replied, and we all rode up to where he was. Barnes came out and asked the news, and shook hands with all but me. Bass said he had none, only that he had Bill Mounts' horse. Barnes replied that he had been very

uneasy about them, since their time was out. 'Why?' said
Bass. 'Well,' said Barnes, 'the news came down here that
one of the Murphy boys was going to give you away, and
I knew you placed a deal of confidence in them.' Bass
replied that he did not reckon it was so. 'They will not
give us away, for Jim is here with us.' 'I tell you,' said
Barnes, 'this news came too straight to be false. I have no
confidence in Jim. I believe we ought to kill him, and
right here; for the marshal telegraphed to Fort Worth
that Jim was going to lead us into Fort Worth to rob a
bank and then lay a plan to catch us. That was the reason
he left Tyler, was to catch us.' Bass replied, 'Well, boys, if
that is the case, we will kill him right here!' I then spoke,
'Well, boys, now I will tell you just how this is: I know
that I agreed to do this with Major Jones, but I had no
notion of doing it. You know that you boys got me into
this trouble, and I fell on that plan to beat the United
States and give Major Jones the grand slip; and I think if
you will take everything into consideration that you will
not kill me.' Frank Jackson then spoke: 'No, Jim, I would
have done the same thing myself.' Barnes exclaimed, 'That
sounds too plagued thin to me, how does it to you, Eph?'
Bass replied, 'I don't know how to fix that up under my
hair. What do you say, Blackey?' 'I have known Jim,'
said Jackson (Blackey), 'for a long time. I know he won't
give me away, nor you either.' Barnes said, 'I think he
will, and we had better kill him.' Bass said, 'All right;
she goes!' Jackson said, 'Well, she don't go; we never eat
her! I tell you, you can't kill Jim without killing me, for
we have persuaded him off from his home, and he said,
the other day, he was afraid that if anything happened
that we would lay it to him. I told him no, that accidents
would crawl upon us now and then anyhow, and that we

would not blame him with them any more than anybody else. So, boys, you must not shoot Jim unless you want h——l to pop; for I will die fighting for him. He is the same as my brother, and you must not hurt him.' Barnes pulled out his pistol and said that he would not trust his brother any more. Frank replied that Jim was a good friend to all of them. Bass replied, 'H——l, h——l! blast the friend! I don't need any friends. They are just friends for my money. Look at Bill Collins: he has gone back on me and I have gone back on everybody. But as Frank is all right, and says that Jim is, I guess we had better let him alone.' So they dropped the subject, and we rode on. We passed through a dark bottom, and I felt alarmed; but Frank and I rode close together all the time. Frank remarked, 'Jim, this is nearly h——l, isn't it?' 'Yes,' I replied. 'Well, I will never let them hurt you, for I know you are all right with me. If you ever lay a plan to catch anybody, you will have some place for me to get out, I know.' 'Yes,' said I, 'that is so, Frank; but I don't want to catch any of them, if they will treat me right.'

"We wound around in the dismal swamp until 12 o'clock that night. We then stopped in an open place and stayed till morning; but it was little rest I got that night. I wished that I was at home several times before I got home. Next morning, after breakfast, Henry Collins and his partner said they were going to a better country than this. Sam spoke to Henry's partner, calling him 'Jake,' and said: 'Jake, you had better come and go with me; I will get you some money. Henry is no thoroughbred; he can't get any money.' Collins replied, 'I know I am no robber, but expect to make plenty of money without robbing.' Bass replied, 'Yes, you will play h——l.' Bass insisted on Jake going with him, but it did no good; he would not go with us. Henry and Jake then left us.

"After their departure Sam remarked: 'What in the h——l do you reckon they aim to do?' Barnes said, 'They think they've got a soft snap somewhere, but I'll bet they slip up on it.' Bass said, 'Yes, the fools will just about step into some old jail, that is what will become of them. Let them go; we'll run our boat and they can run theirs. So, boys, we'll go down the country and cash these old white pistols of ours and get a pretty good roll of greenbacks. Barnes, how much do you think your old white pistol will draw?' 'I don't know,' said Barnes; 'about ten thousand, I guess.' 'H——l! I want at least twenty thousand for mine!' Jackson remarked. 'Well, boys, if you scrubs can get that much, I think Jim and I can draw at least fifty thousand; for we are the best looking. The old banker won't be afraid to trust us.' 'Trust h——l,' said Bass, 'he wouldn't trust any of us if he could help himself. Well, what do you reckon the old banker will say, boys, when we tell him we want to cash these old white pistols?' 'Don't know, Sam, what do you think he will say?' 'Well, I think,' continued Bass, 'when I drop mine up to his ear, he will throw his old top to one side and wall his eyes like a dying calf, and say, "Here are the boys! they want a little money. The cussed old express company can't furnish enough for the boys, and I guess we will have to let them have some money. This must be Colonel Bass. I have heard a heap of talk of him, but I never saw him before." '

"We camped in the edge of East Fork bottom the next night. The musquitoes were so bad here that Jackson made up a small fire close to his head and went to sleep. Next morning his hat was burned up and the tail of his coat gone. Bass enjoyed a hearty laugh over this mishap, in which Frank participated. Mounting his horse, he rode bare headed up to a house near by and bought a hat from a little boy. When he came back, he said they were clever folks up there, and suggested to Bass that they stop and locate there. 'O, no,' said Bass, 'the musquitoes are too big for me here. Let's ride, if your new hat suits you.' 'Ah, yes, it's just a fit,' said Jackson. 'What kind of a Jim Crow story did you tell those folks up there?' inquired Bass. 'O, I told them we were going east to buy cattle,' said Jackson. 'You fool! that is a dead give away. You are too hard a looking case to pass off for a cow man. We had better leave here now, for they will know something is wrong after getting such a gag as that,' said Bass. So we rode out, laughing at Frank's little hat, in the direction of Rockwall.

"When we struck East Fork, it was all over the bottom. There was a bridge across the river, but the water was half side deep to the horses over it. Sam took the lead, and we all followed. Every now and then he would look and say, 'H——l, boys, come on! I will get you out of here, and get you some money.'

"About four o'clock that evening we landed near Rockwall and camped. Barnes was sent up to town to buy some canned fruit, eggs, and salmon. 'Buy everything that is good to eat; that is half my living, is eating,' said Bass. About this time Bass espied a gallows about fifty yards from camp, and exclaimed: 'H——l! Look yonder, boys! If I had seen that before we stopped, we would not have stopped here. Jim, you and Frank get supper, and I will go and look at that blasted thing up yonder.' So he went and took a good look at the gallows. When he came back, he looked very serious, and said, 'Boys, that makes me feel bad; that is the first one of them things I ever saw; and I hope it will be the last.'

"Barnes soon returned with the provisions, and as soon as we could eat we left that camp and went up through Rockwall. As we passed, we stopped at a store and purchased some yeast powders and a sack of table salt. We then went about two miles east from town and camped for the night. The night was very dark and we could not see precisely where we were camping. Bass arose by daybreak next morning and yelled out, 'Boys, get up; look here, we are right at a house! Let's get away from here.'

"We started for Terrell, where we landed about 4 P. M. that day. We camped south of town about one mile. I stopped under two small blackjack trees, and being weary, I soon fell asleep. By some reason Bass and Barnes were still dissatisfied with me and renewed the discussion about my being a spy. Barnes said, 'This is a bad break, boys. I believe there is something wrong. I believe we ought to kill him.' Bass agreed with him, and they drew their pistols and cocked them to blow out my brains while I slept, but Jackson again interposed and saved me. 'You must not do that,' said he. 'Hold up! It will not do. You must not kill him. Kill me first.' This caused them to desist. I knew nothing of this at the time, of course, but learned afterwards from them. Bass and Jackson then went up to town and purchased them some clothing, crackers, and canned peaches. While they were there, they took a look at the banks, but could not tell much about them. Next morning they went back to interview them right. While they were there, they saw Billy Reed (an old acquaintance, and very desperate character), who walked right between them, but did not know them. They both recognized him, and came very near speaking to him, but were afraid he would blow on them. Returning to camp they said they thought they had better hunt better picking. So we left for

Kaufman. Arriving at Kaufman, we camped near, and Bass sent Barnes and I up to town to look for a bank and get some fruit. They found no bank in town. So after getting a new suit of clothes and a shave, we returned to camp. Next morning Bass, Jackson, and I went up to town. Bass and Jackson got shaved, and we had our horses shod and put them up in the livery stable and had them fed. While our horses were eating, we knocked around town and finally we dropped into the best store in town. It was located on the east side of town.

"Bass espied a big safe in the back room, and said, 'Boys, I will test that safe and see if it's any account.' So he threw down a $20 bill to get it broke. The merchant had to go into his safe to get the change. While the old man was getting the change, Bass looked over his shoulder into the safe. When we went out, he said, 'This place is not worth a fig. There was not hardly enough to change that bill. H——l blast such a country as this. Let's go back to camp.' We spent a pleasant evening eating peaches and Bass telling of his troubles and adventures. During the conversation the Dallas and Wichita was mentioned. 'Oh the h——l!' said Bass. 'Now give us a rest! The Dallas and Which-a-way! Now ain't that a bonanza? Well, I would have pulled it, but the poor thing was bogged up in Elm bottom, and I'd as soon hit a woman as to tap it; besides, if I had I'd had to rob the sick thing on a credit, and that won't do in our business.' Bass said to me, 'Jim, what do you think of Tom Gerren?' 'Oh, I always thought Tom was a very good man,' said I. 'Yes, I did too,' said Bass, 'but what do you think of him a-catching of me?' 'Don't know,' I replied, 'I hardly believe he would. I believe he is a good friend.' 'Yes, so do I,' said Bass, 'but he thinks too much of his office to not catch me. Now, I will tell you what I think about it: I think he was

144

a-working to get a down hill pull on me, and me by the heels, and I think he would have pulled me into Uncle Hub Bates' hotel. Oh, blast his soul, I'll always keep a skinned eye on him, you bet, for I know he is nearly h—ll when he gets the drop on a man. And there's that cussed old Judge Hogg. Jim, if I had met him, the old rascal, when he was driving old Coly in his buggy, I would have taken him out and wore my quirt out on him, and then I would have got up into that buggy. I guess I'd have been boss then. What do you reckon he would have said then? Don't you reckon that he would have kicked, but I would drive off the buggy, all the same.' After a pause, Bass sprung to his feet and said: 'Now boys, if that old tree was some old banker, I'll show you how I'd serve him all right. I'd jerk out my pistol and slip up to him, this way, and job it into his countenance. (Going through the evolution of robbing a bank.) Throw up your props, Cap! The old fellow would jump back and say, "Here are the boys; I guess you want some money."' Bass would then approach the tree, with his sack in one hand and his pistol in the other, and shout, 'Hurry up, old man, we are in a hurry.' This performance produced much merriment among the audience.

"Next morning we set out for Ennis and camped that night between Chambers' Creek and East Fork. The following morning we came to Trinidad crossing and found the river up and the cable of the ferry boat broke. We staked out our horses, and Bass and Barnes crossed in a skiff, while Jackson and I put the horses in to swim, but they would not cross. Only swam part of the way and turned down the river and came back. Bass and Barnes returned, and we went to a farmer's house, near by, and spent the 4th of July eating watermelons. Next morning we returned to the crossing and helped them stretch the rope. The ferryman charged us only half fare. We left late in the evening and went to the edge of the bottom and spent the night with a very clever farmer. Bass and he had quite a talk about Bass's gang. We told him that we lived in Wise County, and were wanting to buy some cattle. He said he was looking for Bass to make another strike in that country. He said that it would not surprise him at any time to hear of it; but that he 'didn't care how often Bass robbed railroads, so he let the citizens alone.' Bass said yes, he didn't care much himself, that from what he had heard of Bass he did not believe that Bass would bother anybody except express companies. Bass made a great many inquiries about cattle. Next morning we continued our journey toward Ennis. We met up with a school teacher on the way, and he was very talkative, and we came near not getting rid of him at all. We stopped and bought some watermelons, and the school teacher commenced to count up the cost of them, to see how much was his part. Bass told him that was all right; that he would pay for the whole crowd, that he had plenty of money and didn't care for expenses. Before we got to Ennis, we turned off the road to get rid of the teacher. Bass remarked, 'If he knew he had been traveling with Bass, what would he say?' Jackson said he would tell all of those old bankers to look out—that Bass and Jackson were in and wanted money, and the next thing they would have June Peak down there whooping us up like h——l; that we didn't want any racket until we could make a draw and cash our old white pistols. We stopped about a mile from Ennis. Jackson and Barnes were left in camp while Bass and I went to town and put our horses up in the livery stable, and got our dinner. We then took a view of the bank, but found it bannistered so high that there was no use to try it. Bass here bought and made me a present of a fine cartridge belt, also bought himself a nice pair of small saddle-pockets—the housing was of Cashmere goat skin. Seeing there was nothing here in our line of an inviting character, we set out for Waco. We stopped within one mile of Waco for dinner. Bass sent Jackson and myself into the city to look at the bank. We went, and having provided dinner for ourselves and horses, and got shaved at the barbershop, we struck out to look around town. As we were knocking around, Frank said: 'Jim, this is putting on a heap of style for highwaymen, ain't it?' I replied 'that it was kinder gettin up a little.' Presently we came to the Savings Bank and went in and got a $5 bill changed. While we were in there, we saw a large quantity of gold and greenbacks. Frank said, 'If we mean business, here is the place to commence, Jim.' 'Yes,' said I, 'but here, we must see how we are to get away from here.' 'That's so,' he replied, 'but I don't think there will be any trouble about that.'

"At this we returned to camp and reported. I told Sam that I thought Frank was rather excited over what we saw up there, and that he had better go up and take a look at it himself. So that evening, about dark, we moved on through town and camped just a mile south of town. Next morning Sam and Frank went back to town and looked at the bank again and returned. Sam said: 'Boys, I think we have struck oil, if we will work it right. We will move out five or six miles west of town and rest up our horses.' So we got out in the western suburbs of town. Sam sent me and Frank back to get some coffee and bread, enough to last until we got ready to 'hit the bank.' I suggested to Jackson that we look out a way for retreat when we struck the bank. While we were doing so, I began to point out to Frank where the danger was. Frank said, 'Jim, we will take that just as easy as to take a drink of water. We will scare those town folks so bad that they won't know what is up until we will have the money and be gone.' When we returned to camp, I began to tell where the danger of escape was. Bass said, 'H——l, Jim! we can take that bank just as easy as falling off a log. H——l! don't get scared. I will get you some money in a few days, as soon as old Mounts rests up enough to make a run.' So I thought there was no use talking any more, for they were determined to rob a bank anyhow. So I became very serious, and studied a great deal. Bass would say every now and then, 'H——l, Jim, hold up your head. Keep in good spirits. I will get you some money after awhile.' Next morning, at breakfast, Bass said, 'Well, Jim, if you think there is too much danger here at Waco, we will not hit it. We will go wherever you say.' 'All right, boys,' I replied, 'that is the eddy. I feel better. I was afraid you all would be hard-headed and run yourselves into danger, and get killed. So we will go down to Round Rock and pull the Williamson County Bank.' So after dinner we saddled up and rode back to Waco. Jackson and Barnes went to our old camp, south of the city, while Bass and I stopped at the Ranche Saloon and got some beer. Sam got his last $20 gold piece (the fruits of the U. P. robbery) changed there. As we started off Sam remarked, 'Jim, there goes the last piece of '77 gold I had. It hasn't done me the least bit of good, but that is all right. I will get some more in a few days. So let it gush! It all goes in a lifetime.' We went to the camp and stayed there part of the night and left. Barnes went back to Waco and stole himself a fine bay mare and came on and overtook us. He said, 'Boys, I have got a thoroughbred, that is all right.' Barnes left his old pony with us and told me to sell her at Belton for what we could get. When we reached Belton, I sold her for $25. We then bought some canned fruit and jelly, and went south of Belton, on a high hill, and ate dinner. We could see all over town. Sam said, 'Boys, if that old sheriff knew where we are, he would give us fits, you bet! They whoop little things up, down here. Blamed if I wouldn't hate for them Belton fellows to get after us for they are bad medicine.' Jackson said, 'H——l, Eph, they ain't any worse than old Dad Eagan, and we gave him the grand slip.' 'Yes, but we don't know this country,' replied Bass, 'like we do Denton.' 'I don't give a cuss for that,' said Jackson. 'We know our old Winchesters just as well as we ever did, and I tell you, Eph, whenever we throw red-hot balls at them old Belton fellers, you will see them pull on the bridle reins until their horses can't get out of a walk. Just look at Everheart; he is a brag-fighter, and I tell you when we began to throw red-hot lead at him, you could see his old horse's mouth fly open and stop. That is the way with all of these brag fighters. They blow like h——l, but when they have to face the music they pull upon the bridle, and swear their horse is given out.' 'That is all so, Blackey,' said Sam, 'but I think these Bell County fellows are of different material. I can take a wooden gun and stand Everheart off. He hasn't got as much nerve as Clay Withers, and he hasn't got as much as the law allows him; for when we killed them horses there by Hank's and retreated, if Clay had crowded us right then, he would have caught every one of us, for we were scared, but after we killed the horses, Clay's men did not know but what we might kill some of them next time, and they went kind o' slow. After that it was no trouble to get off. Well, let's be riding; I want to get to Round Rock.'

"At Belton I wrote a letter to Johnson and Everheart, telling them for God's sake, to come at once; that we were bound for Round Rock, to rob the bank there. I slipped this letter in the post office.

"After we had traveled some distance, Sam spoke to me, 'Jim, what do you think of Riley Wetzel for a poker player?' 'Oh, I don't know,' said I. 'I guess he is pretty good.' 'H——l,' said Sam, 'Frank and I met him last spring, and pulled him for all the tax money he had with him at that time. I reckon it was tax money. He said he was out on that kind of business—that he was deputy sheriff. I said, "Well, I guess you would like to collect Bass's crowd and take them in; wouldn't you?" He said that he didn't have any papers for us boys, but *[several words missing from original]* my part of that. You bet I kept a skinned eye on him all the time, for I looked on him just like I did on Gerren. I think all Riley wanted was a down hill pull and running go on my crowd, and I think he would have taken me in just like tax money. But he might have gambled me off before he got to Uncle Hub's hotel. I don't know, though, he might have thought more of me than he did of greenbacks, as I am valuable property. Jim, I would like to be one of those 640 gold interest bearing bonds! If a man could take me alive, he would make a thunder-mug full of money out of me; but that is the point. I never expect to give up to any man alive, for I know it is death anyhow. So I will die a-fighting.'

"We rode into Georgetown, and camping near, rested one day. While here we saw Sheriff Tucker. Sam said: 'Darn his old, long-legged soul, wouldn't he like to know who we are? I expect he would give us a little fight, but it would not do him any good, for he looks too much like some of the crowd that's been after us. He looks like some blow-hard or other, and more of the blow than hard.'

"While at Georgetown, I wrote to Major Jones, that we were on our way to Round Rock, to rob a bank or the railroad, and for God's sake to be on hand and prevent it.

"From Georgetown we went to Round Rock. Frank and Sam first went into town, and came back, saying, 'Jim, you were right about coming to this place, for we can take that bank too easy to talk about.' I agreed with them. We pitched our camp on the San Saba road and went down to old man Mays & Blacks' store, and got some horse feed. Next morning Barnes and I went up to Round Rock to look at the bank and to get shaved. Barnes was well pleased with the town, and said, 'I wish you boys all had fresh horses; we would rob it this evening.' 'Yes,' said I, 'I do, too; but, Sebe, if we go to stealing horses, they will get on to us before we get mounted, and the best thing we can do is to stay here four or five days and let our horses rest, and pretend that we want to buy cattle.' Barnes said, 'Yes, Jim, that is the idea.' After we got back to camp, Barnes said, 'Boys, I am satisfied that Jim is all right. I am glad that Frank kept us from killing him; he is old business. He has traveled around enough to make a good appearance in town. He is the man that we need, but blast him I could not fix him all right before; but I am glad he is with us now! I think if we will keep low, we will get seven or eight thousand dollars.'

" 'Well, now boys, she goes,' said Sam, 'about half-past 3 o'clock, Saturday evening. Now, we will talk over our plans, and understand what every fellow has to do.' 'All right, Sam,' was the reply, 'you lay out the plans, and we will work to them, as you understand the business better than anybody else.'

" 'All right,' said Sam. 'Now I will tell you how we will do. Bass and Barnes will walk in first. Barnes will throw down a $5 bill and tell the banker that he wants silver for it, and while he is getting the change, I, Bass, will walk in, throw my pistol down on him, and tell him to throw up his props. Barnes will jump over the counter, and Jim and Frank will stand in the door, and if anybody else comes to deposit, they can arrest them and take their money and give them a certificate of deposit, and tell them to stand there until their partners come out, for they think that Eph has got some relations, and he told us if we saw you to have you be sure and wait for him—he has some business to talk about with you. Tell them there's no use kicking, for that I am bound to see them. Say to him, just stand still, young man, your Uncle Eph will be here directly.' But as good luck was with the citizens, Sam did not get to carry out his plan. We stayed there until Friday evening, when we all concluded to go up to town to get some tobacco. I told them that I would stop at Old Round Rock. They went up to the New Town. As they got off their horses, Sam's coat tail blew up and exposed his pistol. Frank and Sebe had theirs in their saddle-pockets, and if Sam had had his in his saddle-pockets he might have been living yet. A deputy sheriff saw Sam's pistol, and followed in after him, and while in the store, the deputy sheriff thought he would take the pistol away, and it resulted in the death of the deputy sheriff. When the deputy sheriff was killed by them, Sam and Frank got on their horses, and came back through Old Rock, and passed right close to me, and I thought they looked at me, but Frank says they did not see me. I was sitting in old man Mays' store when they passed. I saw that Sam was wounded in the hand, and he looked like he was sick, and Frank was holding him on his horse, the last I saw of them."

CHAPTER XVI

Fate Does Its Work

The death of Bass and Barnes at Round Rock—Murphy
redeems his promise and wins his reward
—Jackson alone escapes

T HE LETTER written by Murphy at Belton was received in due time by Major Jones, and he went instantly to Round Rock, taking with him Maurice Moore, deputy sheriff of Travis County, to make preparations to bag the robbers. A detachment of state Rangers, under Lieutenant Reynolds, was ordered to the same point, and Lieutenant Arnold, with another detachment of Rangers, was commanded to hurry across from San Saba.

Having arrived at Round Rock, Major Jones notified the banker what was up, and put him on his guard, giving him also information of the measures he had taken to circumvent the bandits. These measures, as was shown in Murphy's narrative, miscarried, by the precipitancy of Deputy Sheriff Moore, who, in his statement, said: "I saw these men dismount, and noticed that one of them had a pistol on. I watched them as they walked up the street from their horses, and they looked at me rather hard, and went across the street into a store. I walked up the street to where Grimes, the deputy sheriff of Williamson County, was standing, and remarked to him, 'I think one of those men has a six-shooter on.' Grimes remarked that he would look and see. We walked across the street and went into the store. Not wishing to let them know I was watching them, I stood up inside the store door with my hands in my pockets, whistling. Grimes approached them carelessly and asked one if he had not a six-shooter. They all three replied, 'Yes,' and at the same instant two of them shot Grimes and one shot me.

"After I had fired my first shot, I could not see the men on account of the smoke. They continued shooting, and so did I, until I fired five shots. As they passed out, I saw one man bleeding from the arm and side; I then leaned against the store door, feeling faint and sick, and recovering myself, I started on and fired the remaining shot at one of them.

"Having lent one of my pistols to another man the day before, I stopped and reloaded my pistol, went into the stable, and got my Winchester and started in pursuit of them, and was stopped by Dr. Morris, who said, 'Hold on; don't go any further, for if you get overheated your wound may kill you.' I stopped and gave my Winchester to another man. Grimes did not have time to pull out his pistol; six bullet holes were put through his body.

"The Rangers, hearing the firing, came upon the scene and fired upon the robbers as they retreated. Major Jones reached the place in time to engage in the fusillade. The whole village was thrown into a tumult of excitement, and the citizens, who could procure arms, joined in the affray. The robbers taking cover behind houses and fences, and firing back at every opportunity, retreated down an alley towards their horses. Early in the engagement Bass had received a shot through the hand, and as they retreated down the alley, a Ranger, George Harrall, shot him in the back, inflicting a mortal wound. He, however, reached and mounted his horse. Barnes was shot by Geo. Ware, a Ranger, through the head, just as he mounted his horse, and fell dead on the spot. Jackson and Bass rode off together. Major Jones, Ware, and Tubbs fired at them as they left. F. L. Jordan and Albert Highsmith, citizens of Round Rock, joined in the fight and did their best to lift the robbers out of their saddles. Major Jones, Captain Lee Hall, and three Rangers gave chase on horseback, but the bandits had the start of them too far, and they lost the trail and returned to the town. That evening Lieutenant Reynolds with ten Rangers, from San Saba, and Lieutenant Armstrong, from Austin, with a squad, arrived at Round Rock. After Bass and Jackson had gone several miles from the scene, Bass's wounds began to grow so sore that he found he would have to stop. Jackson wanted to stop and remain with him, but Bass told him no—that he was seriously wounded and must stop, and that Frank must take care of himself. He gave Jackson all the money he had, his horse, arms, and ammunition and enjoined him to go and leave him. Jackson took his departure from Bass and left him there alone. After Jackson left, Bass went to a house to get some water. He was bloody and looked very feeble; this attracted the attention of the lady of the house who gave him the water. After he got the water, he left afoot and the lady saw the direction he went. Next morning she informed his pursuers of the incident and by this means he was found. We give below, an extract from a letter from Travis County, written to the *Galveston News* and clipped from the *Denton Monitor* of August 2d, '78 as follows:

"Later in the evening Lieut. Armstrong's party from Austin arrived. Next morning Sergt. Neville, of Lieut. Reynold's company, with eight men and Deputy Sheriff

Tacker, of this county, took the trail of Bass and Jackson where it had been lost the evening before, but soon found that the two had separated.

"After hunting around a while they found Bass lying under a large tree in the edge of the prairie. As the sergeant approached, he held up his hand and said, 'Don't shoot; I am unarmed and helpless; I am the man you're looking for; I am Sam Bass.'

"He had lain in the brush all night, but crawled out to the tree in the prairie about daylight, and hailed a Negro who was passing him, and tried to bribe him to haul him off and secrete him. Information of the capture was brought to Major Jones, who went out, accompanied by Dr. Cochran, and brought the prisoner in.

"Of the seven men who were engaged in the train robbery at Mesquite, on the Texas and Pacific Railroad, on the 10th of April last, some of whom were in all the robberies which took place on the Texas Central, and T. P. railroads, previous to that time, five had been disposed of. Sam Pipes and Albert Herndon, arrested by Major Jones and Captain Peak, in Dallas County, soon after the robbery occurred, have just been convicted in the federal court at Austin. Johnson, called "Arkansaw," was killed by Sergeant Floyd, of Captain Peak's company, in the fight with the robbers on Sale Creek, in Wise County, on the 12th of June. Sam Bass and Seaborn Barnes were killed by R. C. Ware and Henry Harreil (as per convict coroner's jury), of Lieutenant Reynolds' company, at Round Rock, on the 10th of July, 1878. Two of the band are still at large—Frank Jackson, who made his escape at Round Rock, and Henry Underwood, who left the band at the time of the Salt Creek fight, and has not been with them since, and of whom nothing is certainly known since that time."

Every endeavor was made by Major Jones to secure Bass's confession. Someone was nearly always near him with pencil and paper to take down what he had to say. In his moments of wakefulness he talked guardedly to Dr. Cochran, his nurse Jim Chatman, Major Jones, and some of the Rangers. His utterances, though not really of great moment, are yet valuable and interesting; are disjointed and tempered with a reserve that is tantalizing. A book was kept to jot down his sayings in. From this book we copy verbatim: "Joel Collins, Bill Heffridge, Tom Nixon, Jack Davis, Jim Berry and me were in the Union Pacific robbery. Tom Nixon is in Canada; haven't seen him since that robbery. Jack Davis was in New Orleans from the time of the Union Pacific robbery till he went to Denton to get me to go in with him and buy hides. This was the last of April, 1878.

"Grimes asked if I had a pistol. Said I had, and then all three of us drew and shot him. If I killed him, he was the first man I ever killed. Am 25 years old, and have two brothers, John and Linton; have four sisters. They all live at Mitchell, Ind. Have not seen Henry Underwood since the Salt Creek fight. Saw the two Collinses at old man Collins', since I left Denton.

"Gardner, living in Atascosa County is my friend. Was at his house last fall. Went to Kansas with him once. Have been in the robbing business a long time. Had done much of that kind of business before the U.P. robbery last fall.

"First time I saw Billy Scott was at Bob Murphy's; last time was at Green Hill's. Saw him at William Collins', but do not know the date; do not pay any attention to dates. Never saw him but those three times. I will not tell who was in the Eagle Ford robbery besides myself and Jackson, because it is against my profession. Think I will go to hell, anyhow, and believe a man should die with what he knows in him.

"I do not know. [Question as to whereabouts of certain confreres—Rep.] They were with us about six months. Henry was with me in the Salt Creek fight, four or five weeks ago. Arkansaw Johnson was killed in that fight. Do not know whether Underwood was wounded in the Salt Creek fight or not. Sebe Barnes, Frank Jackson and Charley Carter were there. We were all set afoot in that fight, but stole horses enough to remount ourselves in three hours, or as soon as dark came, after which we went back to Denton, where we stayed till we came to Round Rock."

Q—"Where is Jackson, now?"

A—"I do not know."

Q—"How did you usually get together after being scattered?"

A—"Generally told by friends." [Declined to tell who these friends were.]

Q—"How came you to commence this kind of life?"

A—"Started out on sporting horses."

Q—"Why did you get worse than horse-racing?"

A—"Because they robbed me of my first $300."

Q—"After they robbed you, what did you do next?"

A—"Went to robbing stages in Black Hills—robbed seven. Got very little money. Jack Davis, Nixon, and myself were all that were in the Black Hills stage robberies."

Speaking of Bass's caution in not compromising himself or his friends, Major Jones, who had him in charge, says: "I tried every conceivable plan to obtain some information from him, but to no purpose. About noon on Sunday, he began to suffer greatly and sent for me to know if I could not give him some relief. I did everything I could for him.

Thinking this an excellent opportunity, I said to him, 'Bass, you have done much wrong in this world, you now have an opportunity to do some good before you die by giving some information which will lead to the vindication of that justice which you have so often defied and the law which you have constantly violated.' He replied, 'No, I won't tell.' 'Why won't you?' said I. 'Because it is agin my profession to blow on my pals. If a man knows anything, he ought to die with it in him.' He positively refused to converse on religion, and in reply to some remark made, he said, 'I am going to hell anyhow.' I made a particular effort to obtain some information from him in regard to William Collins. I asked him if he was ever at Collins' house. He said no. I then put the question in a different form, saying, 'Where did you first see Will Scott?' He replied, at Bob Murphy's. I then said, 'You saw him at Green Hill's too, didn't you?' He replied, yes. These answers were not of any consequence, but I then said, 'When did you see him at William Collins'?' He said, 'I don't remember, as I never paid any attention to dates, being always on the scout, I only saw him these three times.' This answer was important, as it fixed the fact that Bass was at Collins' house. But this was the only statement of any importance which he made. All the other statements were of facts well known or concerning individuals beyond the reach of future justice."

Bass clung to the hope of life to the last extremity. While suffering the most excruciating anguish from his wounds, he hugged the delusion of recovery. At last when his physician told him that death was fast approaching, and that he would soon be gone to eternity he said, "Let me go!" Then closing his eyes for a few moments, he opened them and exclaimed to his nurse, as if startled, "The world is bobbing around me!"

CHAPTER XVII

The End Cometh

Death of Henry Collins—Billie Collins and Deputy
United States Marshal Wm. Anderson kill
each other—Some reflections

A S HAS BEEN before stated, Henry Collins, the brother of
Joel Collins, the leader in the Union Pacific robbery
and of Billie Collins, was also charged with being connected with Bass and his outlaws. From all the evidence
in the case, it is not believed now that he was directly
connected with the bandits. His brother Billie made several
trips to the encampment of Bass in Denton County,
spending some days there on each occasion, and was the
recipient of $1,800 from Bass in $20 gold pieces taken
from the Express Company at Big Springs. Billie was also
a participant in the Mesquite robbery, and Henry doubtless knew of his brother's visits to Bass, and also knew of
the Mesquite robbery before it took place. In fact, he
argued and pleaded with his brother and with Pipes and
Herndon to have nothing to do with the Mesquite affair,
refusing himself to countenance it, or participate in it. He
probably knew after the facts of the Allen, Hutchins, and
Eagle Ford robberies and knew who composed the Bass
band, gaining the knowledge from his brother, Pipes,
Herndon, and Seaborn Barnes, who after being wounded at
Mesquite remained some days at the house of Billie Collins.

The End Cometh

To the extent of the knowledge, and to the extent of going to Bass and joining his fortunes with those of the outlaw after the officers of the law were after him, he was guilty and no further.

At the Salt Creek fight in Wise County where "Arkansaw" Johnson was killed, Henry Collins left Bass and was never seen by the outlaw again. This was in May, 1878, and from that time until in the September following, his whereabouts were unknown to the officers who were on the watch for him. Where he went or what he did is unknown except to his family and some of his friends perhaps.

Better would it have been for him and for his parents and relatives, had he during this time, sought a home in some distant part of the country and under an assumed name sunk his identity, waiting for time to right him and make known all the facts in the case. But fate had decreed otherwise. He was the youngest boy and his heart clung to the loving mother, the fond father whose joy he had ever been, and longings for the dear old homestead where he had always been so happy and where joy had reigned so supreme, filled and swayed his heart and he could not stay away, but must needs linger near, where at least he could now and then catch a gleam of the old-time sunshine, and feel its warmth.

In September the officers of Sherman learned that Henry was at the house of a relative of his in Grayson County, visiting, They at once set about to effect his capture, and a posse with a deputy sheriff of the county and Sam Ball, marshal of Sherman, proceeded to the house in question. They found Henry near the place, and commanding him to surrender, he refused and a fight ensued. Henry killed a horse belonging to one of the posse and was himself shot in the leg, the bone being broken so that he could not escape, and then he surrendered. He was forthwith conveyed to Sherman and lodged in jail. A physician being called to attend to his wounds, decided that amputation was necessary to save his life. The operation was performed, but the weather being warm, gangrene set in and the unfortunate died in the prison, in less than a week after he was shot. His mother and father and other relatives were with him and did all that loving care and attention could to assuage his pain and save his life, but in vain.

It is due to the parents of Henry, Billie, and Joel Collins to say here, that better, more upright people do not live in this country than they are. They are Christians: good citizens, enjoying the esteem and confidence of all who know them. They raised their children up in the paths of virtue and rectitude, impressing them with their duty to God, to the laws of the land and to the fellow-men. And the brothers and sisters of these young men now living, are good men and women; upright in all the walks of life: influential in their respective communities and well-to-do in the world and honored where they live.

Billie Collins, who undoubtedly was *particeps criminis* in the Mesquite robbery and who was accessory after the fact in all the other train robberies, unless it was the one at Allen Station, and who was in all probability accessory before the fact, also, in the Hutchins and Eagle Ford robberies, fled the country shortly after the culmination of affairs in Denton County described in preceding chapters.

He had been taken in charge at his home in Dallas County, as a witness, and taken under guard to Tyler, where he found an indictment against him for participation in the Mesquite robbery. He was lodged in jail, but being able to give bond, was released on bail in the sum of $10,000. He then returned home and began secretly his preparations for flight, and about the time that Bass, Jackson, and Jim Murphy left Denton County on their tour so graphically pictured by Murphy in his story, or a little afterwards, he left for parts unknown.

Deputy United States Marshal William Anderson, a shrewd, active officer who had figured somewhat, in a quiet way, in the campaign against the marauders, set about to discover his whereabouts. To this end he watched the post office, and through letters from Collins to his wife, who was still at his home in Dallas County, he learned that Collins was in the British possessions, at some point near the Dakota Territory line. Having sent a decoy letter to get Collins across the line into Dakota Territory, he left Dallas on Tuesday, October 29th, 1878, for Pembina, a small town in said territory, but a few miles from the British line. On the 6th or 7th, Anderson arrived at Pembina and proceeded to look around very secretly for his man. He learned that Collins had been at work for a farmer a few miles from Pembina, helping him to save hay, but having left that employment, he had gone to work in Pembina, under an assumed name of course, keeping bar in a small saloon.

Anderson, on the 8th of November, repaired to the post office in Pembina and taking position on the inside of the office in the private apartments of the postmaster, he sent an officer of the town to inveigle Collins into the post office. He waited some time, but it seems the officer did not for some cause succeed in his mission, and Anderson had well nigh given up that plan, when he happened to see Collins enter the post office. On the instant he left his position and approached Collins, getting within a few feet of him before he was perceived, and just as Collins looked up from the letter box in which he had deposited a letter, he presented his cocked six-shooter in his face with the command, "Hold up your hands! You are my prisoner." Collins smiled and complied, remarking, "How are you, Billie?" He immediately dropped his right hand and threw it on his pistol and as he attempted to draw it, Anderson fired, his pistol being not over a foot from Collins' breast and the ball passed through Collins' heart. Anderson then ran a distance of some twenty feet and dodged through a door leading into the postmaster's private room, where he had just been on the watch for Collins. When Collins was shot, he did not change countenance, but with a smile still on his face he fired at Anderson as he ran, missing him. Collins then stepped to the left a yard or more beside a stove, pistol still in hand and watching the door. After Anderson had dodged through the door, he returned to it to look out and see what had become of Collins, knowing that he had shot him. As he stepped into the door, Collins fired again on the instant, his ball passing through Anderson's heart and both men fell dead, on the spot.

The first news of the affair received in Dallas was on the morning of the 9th of November, when the following dispatch was received by the Texas Express Company:

St. Paul, Minn. Nov. 9th, 1878.

To agents of the Texas Express Company:

W. H. Anderson, Deputy U. S. Marshal, was shot dead at Pembina, Dakota Territory, last night, by William Collins. The officer got the drop on Collins, who drew his revolver. Anderson then shot him. Collins not being killed instantly, shot twice and killed Anderson. Both men died in two minutes. Notify express officials, and instruct us what to do with the remains.

J. E. Atherton,
Route Agent American Express Company.

Collins was buried at Pembina, but the body of Anderson was sent for and brought to Dallas by his family and friends, and interred in the cemetery in that city.

The bondsmen of Collins sent on to Pembina two agents, Mr. George Waller and Mr. Lida Huffman, both of Dallas, to identify the body of Collins, that they might be released from their bond in the United States court. These gentlemen, when they reached Pembina, had the body disinterred at great trouble, as the ground was entirely frozen, and knew the corpse to be that of Billie Collins, as no decomposition, owing to the extreme cold weather, had taken place at all. They had photographs of the body taken, which they brought back with them.

It is due to the Express Company to say that it paid to the widow of Anderson the reward they had offered for his apprehension.

Thus it will be seen that connection with Sam Bass had caused the death and disgrace of three members of the same family, Joel Collins, Billie Collins, and Henry Collins, and brought a sorrow upon their aged parents, from the shadow of which they will never emerge this side of the grave. There remains little more to be said. Bass, the three Collins boys, Arkansaw Johnson, Seaborn Barnes, Berry, and Heffridge, all with the black stain of crime upon their names and their memories, sleep in bloody graves, and Deputy Sheriff Grimes, of Williamson County, and Deputy Marshal William H. Anderson, faithful officers of the law and guardians of the peace, are also sleeping their last sleep in ensanguined cerements, the price of their devotion to duty in upholding the law and striving to protect their fellow citizens from rapine and wrong. May the fearful ends of these outlaws prove to be effective warnings to all who are ever tempted to wander from the road right and to outrage the sanctity of God's law, the majesty of the laws of the land. Virtue has its reward in a clear conscience, in the approving smiles of Heaven, and in the respect, the confidence and the good will of one's fellow men, while wrong and crime carry with them their penalties of disgrace, infamy, and death. The flowers of earth may bloom with all their brightness over the graves of Bass and his bandits, and the grass of spring have all its luxuriance, but the brightness of the one and the emerald of the other, will ever a thrill of horror cause, to those who see them, and though there be hearts that ache and tears that flow because they are no more and because of their reckless, bad lives, the ground that hides them is banned, is forsaken of all the earth.

Jim Murphy the informer, after having the cases against him dismissed, returned to Denton, but did not live long. He was attacked with sore eyes and the physician prescribing atropia, he was poisoned by it and died in convulsions.